JavaScript Code

Foundations for Beginners

Unlock Your Potential with Practical Coding

Challenges

By

Laurence Lars Svekis

Dedicated to

Alexis and Sebastian

Thank you for your support

For more content and to learn more, visit

https://basescripts.com/

2

3

Introduction

Welcome to **JavaScript Code Foundations for Beginners**, a hands-on guide designed to transform your coding potential into practical skills. This book is more than just a collection of programming exercises—it's a pathway to mastering core JavaScript concepts through interactive, real-world challenges.

Whether you're just beginning your journey or looking to solidify your foundational knowledge, this book is structured to cater to learners of all levels. Each chapter builds upon the previous one, ensuring a smooth progression as you develop your programming expertise.

Why Coding Matters

In the 21st century, coding is not just a technical skill—it's a form of literacy. From creating websites and automating tasks to powering the apps and tools we use daily, coding lies at the heart of innovation. Learning to code:

- **Empowers creativity:** Build your ideas into functional applications.
- **Enhances problem-solving:** Approach challenges with a logical mindset.

- **Opens career opportunities:** Programming skills are highly sought after across industries.
- **Provides versatility:** JavaScript, the focus of this book, is used everywhere—from web browsers to servers.

What This Book Offers

Practical Learning

This book isn't about memorizing concepts; it's about applying them. Each chapter introduces a programming topic, followed by exercises that let you explore the concept in depth.

Step-by-Step Guidance

Every exercise is accompanied by clear explanations and solutions, ensuring you understand the "why" behind every piece of code.

Real-World Scenarios

The exercises simulate real-world problems, helping you gain skills you can use immediately in personal or professional projects.

Progressive Challenges

Exercises range from beginner to intermediate levels, offering incremental challenges that help you grow confidently.

How This Book Is Structured

Each chapter focuses on a key JavaScript concept, providing:

1. **Concept Overview:** A concise explanation of the topic.
2. **Code Examples:** Illustrations of how the concept is applied.
3. **Exercises:** A series of coding challenges, each building on the last.
4. **Multiple-Choice Questions:** Review questions to reinforce your understanding.

Here's a glimpse of what you'll learn:

- **Variables and Constants:** Storing and managing data in your programs.
- **Data Types:** Understanding strings, numbers, booleans, and more.
- **Basic Operators:** Performing calculations, comparisons, and logical operations.
- **Conditional Statements:** Making decisions in your code.
- **Loops:** Repeating tasks efficiently.
- **Functions:** Writing reusable, modular code.
- **DOM Manipulation:** Interacting with web pages dynamically.
- **Event Handling:** Responding to user interactions.

- **Form Management:** Handling and validating user input.

Who Is This Book For?

This book is designed for:

- **Beginners:** Anyone starting their coding journey and looking for a hands-on approach.
- **Self-Learners:** Individuals who prefer to learn by doing, rather than solely through theory.
- **Educators:** Teachers seeking structured exercises for their students.
- **Career Changers:** Professionals looking to pivot into tech with a solid foundation in JavaScript.

What You'll Need

To make the most of this book, you'll need:

- A computer with internet access.
- A modern web browser (Google Chrome, Firefox, or Edge).
- A text editor or IDE, such as Visual Studio Code.
- A willingness to experiment, fail, and learn.

How to Approach This Book

1. **Start Sequentially:** Chapters are arranged to build on each other. Begin with Chapter 1 and progress step by step.
2. **Code Along:** Don't just read—type out the examples and exercises. Modify the code to see how it changes the outcome.
3. **Challenge Yourself:** Tackle each exercise with curiosity and determination. Struggling is part of the learning process.
4. **Use the Review Questions:** Test your understanding at the end of each chapter to reinforce what you've learned.

Your Journey Begins Now

Embarking on the path to becoming a proficient programmer is both challenging and rewarding. By the time you finish this book, you'll have the foundational knowledge and hands-on experience to tackle real-world programming challenges confidently.

Coding is a skill that grows with practice, and this book is your companion for taking the first steps. So, let's dive in, write some code, and start building the future!

Fundamental JavaScript Concepts

JavaScript Variables and Constants

Introduction

Variables allow us to store and manipulate data in our programs. In JavaScript, we have three main keywords for variable declaration:

`var`

`let`

`const`

`var` (Function-scoped or Global-scoped)

Historically the main way to declare variables (pre-ES6). Its scope is either function-level or global if declared outside a function.

Can be redeclared and updated.

```
var x = 10;
console.log(x); // 10
function exampleVar() {
 var y = 20;
 console.log(y); // 20
}
```

exampleVar();

// y is not accessible here (outside the function)

`let` (Block-scoped)

Introduced in ES6 (2015).

Has block scope: accessible only within the nearest set of curly braces `{ ... }`.

Can be updated but not redeclared in the same scope.

```
let a = 5;
a = 7;
console.log(a); // 7
if (true) {
let b = 10;
 console.log(b); // 10
}
// b is not accessible outside the if-block
```

`const` (Block-scoped constant)

Introduced in ES6.

Similar to `let` but the value cannot be reassigned once declared (though object properties can still be mutated).

Must be initialized at the time of declaration.

```
const PI = 3.14159;
console.log(PI); // 3.14159
// PI = 3.14; // Error: Assignment to constant variable.
```

Hoisting

Declarations (`var`, `let`, and `const`) are hoisted
to the top of their scope, but only `var`
declarations are initialized with `undefined`.
`let` and `const` remain in a "temporal dead zone" until they
are declared.

Example of hoisting with `var`:

console.log(hoistedVar); //
undefined (var is hoisted but not yet
assigned) var hoistedVar = 10;

With `let`:

// console.log(notHoistedLet); // ReferenceError:
Cannot access 'notHoistedLet' before initi alization
let notHoistedLet = 20;

25 Multiple-Choice Questions: Variables and Constants

1. Which keyword is block-scoped in JavaScript?

A. `var`

B. `let`

C. `function`

D. `global`

Answer: B

Explanation: `let` and `const` are block-scoped,
whereas `var` is function-scoped or global scoped.

2. **Which keyword can be redeclared in the same scope without error?**

A. `var`

B. `let`

C. `const`

D. `function`

Answer: A

Explanation: A variable declared with `var` can be redeclared, though it's generally considered bad practice.

3. **Which keyword cannot be reassigned a new value after initialization?**

A. `var`

B. `let`

C. `const`

D. `global`

Answer: C

Explanation: `const` declares a read-only reference to a value; it cannot be reassigned.

4. **What happens if you try to log a `let` variable before it is declared?**

A. Outputs `undefined`

B. Throws a `ReferenceError`

C. Throws a `TypeError`

D. Automatically initializes to `null`

Answer: B

Explanation: Accessing a `let` variable before its declaration results in a `ReferenceError` due to the temporal dead zone.

5. **What is the default initialization of a `var` variable during the creation phase?**

A. `null`

B. `undefined`

C. 0

D. Throws an error

Answer: B

Explanation: `var` is hoisted and initializes to `undefined` before the assignment.

6. **Which of the following is true about `const` in JavaScript?**

A. It can be declared without an initial value.

B. It can be reassigned any time.

C. It must be initialized at declaration.

D. It is function-scoped.

Answer: C

Explanation: `const` must be initialized at the time of declaration.

7. Which of the following accurately describes hoisting of `let`?

A. It is hoisted and assigned the value `undefined`.

B. It is not hoisted at all.

C. It is hoisted, but in the temporal dead zone until the declaration.

D. It is hoisted and immediately assigned its declared value.

Answer: C

Explanation: `let` is hoisted but can't be accessed until its declaration, leading to a temporal dead zone.

8. Which of the following is NOT a valid variable name in JavaScript?

A. `_result`

B. `$variable`

C. `2count`

D. `camelCase`

Answer: C

Explanation: Variable names cannot start with a digit.

9. Which of the following statements about `var` is false?

A. It is function-scoped.

B. It can be redeclared.

C. It can be used before its declaration without error.

D. It can never store `undefined`.

Answer: D

Explanation: `var` can store `**undefined**`. In fact, it is initially assigned `**undefined**` when hoisted.

10. **Which operator is used to assign a value to a variable in JavaScript?**

A. `==`

B. `=`

C. `===`

D. `!=`

Answer: B

Explanation: The single equals sign `=` is the assignment operator.

11. **Which statement about `const` objects is correct?**

A. They cannot have their properties changed.

B. They can be re-declared.

C. They can have their properties mutated.

D. They must always be integers.

Answer: C

Explanation: A `**const**` object's reference can't change, but its internal properties can be modified.

12. **Choose the correct way to declare a variable using ES6 block scope syntax: A. `block score = 10;`**

B. `var score = 10;`

C. `let score = 10;`

D. `block var score = 10;`

Answer: C

Explanation: `let` is the correct ES6 block-scoped declaration.

13. **What is the scope of a variable declared with `var` inside a function?**

A. Global scope

B. Block scope

C. Function scope

D. Lexical scope

Answer: C

Explanation: `var` declared inside a function is scoped to that function.

14. **What will be logged to the console?**

```
function testVar() {
  console.log(myVar);
  var myVar = 5;
}
testVar();
```

A. 5

B. `undefined`

C. `ReferenceError`

D. `TypeError`

Answer: B

Explanation: Because of hoisting, `myVar` is declared at the top of the function and initialized to `undefined`.

15. **Which variable declaration allows you to change its value later?**

A. `const x = 5; x = 6;`

B. `let x = 5; x = 6;`

C. `var x = 5; const x = 6;`

D. `let x = 5; const x = 6;`

Answer: B

Explanation: `let` can be reassigned, while `const` cannot.

16. **Which is a correct reason to prefer `let` or `const` over `var`?**

A. They are older.

B. They are not hoisted.

C. They reduce accidental redeclaration and have clearer scope.

D. They are faster than `var` in all browsers.

Answer: C

Explanation: `let` and `const` reduce scope-related bugs and accidental redeclarations.

17. **Which of the following is a valid ES6 declaration?**

A. `let 2x = 10;`

B. `const x = 10; x = 20;`

C. `let x = 10;`

D. `let function = 'test';`

Answer: C

Explanation: Variable names cannot start with a digit or use reserved keywords, and `const` cannot be reassigned.

18. **If you don't initialize a `var` variable, what is its initial value?**

A. `undefined`

B. `null`

C. 0

D. `ReferenceError`

Answer: A

Explanation: A `var` variable is initialized to `undefined` if not assigned.

19. **What is the best practice for declaring variables in modern JavaScript?** A. Always use `var`.

B. Use `let` or `const` depending on whether reassignment is needed.

C. Use `let` for everything, never `const`.

D. Use `const` for all variables, including those that need to change.

Answer: B

Explanation: It's best to use `const` whenever possible for immutable references, and `let` for variables that need to change.

20. **Which will NOT cause a syntax error?**

A. `let x = 10; let x = 20;`

B. `var x = 10; var x = 20;`

C. `const x = 10; x = 20;`

D. `let 123x = 10;`

Answer: B

Explanation: Redeclaring a variable with `var` in the same scope is allowed, although it's not recommended.

21. **What will be the result of running this code?**

console.log(myVar);

var myVar = 30;

A. Logs `30`

B. Logs `undefined`

C. Throws `ReferenceError`

D. Throws `TypeError`

Answer: B

Explanation: `var` is hoisted and initialized to `undefined` before assignment.

22. **Which declaration is most appropriate for a constant that won't change?** A. `var TAX_RATE = 0.07;`

B. `let TAX_RATE = 0.07;`

C. `const TAX_RATE = 0.07;`

D. `variable TAX_RATE = 0.07;`

Answer: C

Explanation: `const` is used for values that should not change.

23. **Why might you prefer `let` over `var`?**

A. `let` is universally supported by all old browsers.

B. `let` has function scope, which is more convenient.

C. `let` has block scope, reducing scope-related issues.

D. `var` is faster than `let`.

Answer: C

Explanation: Block scope can help avoid unintentional variable leaks.

24. **Which will throw an error?**

const x = 5;

x = 10;

A. It will log `5`.

B. It will log `10`.

C. It will throw a `ReferenceError`.

D. It will throw a `TypeError`.

Answer: D

Explanation: Reassignment to a `const` variable throws a `TypeError`.

25. **Which variable is NOT in scope in the line `console.log(num);`?**

```
if (true) {
  let num = 42;
}
console.log(num);
```

A. `num` is in the global scope.

B. `num` is in block scope, so `console.log(num);` fails.

C. `num` is function-scoped.

D. `num` is undefined by default.

Answer: B

Explanation: `let` within an `if` block is block-scoped. Outside that block, `num` is not accessible.

JavaScript Data Types

Introduction

JavaScript has several built-in data types. The most commonly used include:

String: A sequence of characters (`"Hello"`, `"World"`, or `Template literal`).

Number: Integers or floating-point numbers (e.g., `42`, `3.14`, `Infinity`, `NaN`). **Boolean**: Represents a logical entity with two values: `true` or `false`.

Null: A special keyword denoting a null value (explicitly nothing).

Undefined: A variable that has been declared but not assigned a value.

BigInt: For large integers beyond the safe integer range (`Number.MAX_SAFE_INTEGER`). **Symbol**: A unique, immutable identifier.

String Examples

```
let greeting = "Hello, World!";
let singleQuoteStr = 'Single quotes';
let templateLiteral = `Hello, ${greeting}`;
```

Number Examples

```
let integerNum = 10;
let floatNum = 3.14;
let bigNumber = 1.23e9; // 1.23 * 10^9
let notANumber = NaN; // Not a Number
```

Boolean Examples

```
let isActive = true;
let isComplete = false;
```

Special Types

let unknownValue = null; // explicitly nothing

let uninitialized; // implicitly undefined

console.log(uninitialized); // undefined

Type Checking

Use `typeof` to check the data type:

console.log(typeof "hello"); // "string"

console.log(typeof 42); // "number"

console.log(typeof true); // "boolean"

console.log(typeof undefined); // "undefined"

console.log(typeof null); // "object" (known quirk in JavaScript)

console.log(typeof Symbol("id")); // "symbol"

25 Multiple-Choice Questions: Data Types

1. Which of the following is NOT a JavaScript data type?

A. String

B. Number

C. Boolean

D. Character

Answer: D

Explanation: JavaScript does not have a separate "Character" type; characters are simply strings of length 1.

2. Which operator can check a variable's data type?

A. `typeof`

B. `instanceof`

C. `type`

D. `datatype`

Answer: A

Explanation: `typeof` returns a string indicating the type of the operand.

3. **What is the result of `typeof null` in JavaScript?**

A. `"null"`

B. `"object"`

C. `"undefined"`

D. `"string"`

Answer: B

Explanation: Due to a historical bug in JavaScript, `typeof null` returns `"object"`.

4. **Which statement is true about `NaN` in JavaScript?**

A. It is equivalent to 0.

B. It is a number type.

C. It is a string.

D. It is a boolean type.

Answer: B

Explanation: `NaN` (Not a Number) is of the type `number` in JavaScript.

5. **Which is the correct way to initialize a string in**

JavaScript?

A. `let str = "Hello";`

B. `let str = 'Hello';`

C. `let str = `Hello`;`

D. All of the above

Answer: D

Explanation: JavaScript strings can be enclosed in double quotes, single quotes, or backticks. 6. **What is the value of `typeof []` (an empty array)?**

A. `"array"`

B. `"object"`

C. `"undefined"`

D. `"null"`

Answer: B

Explanation: Arrays in JavaScript are a type of object, so `typeof []` returns `"object"`.

7. **Which data type can store large integers beyond `Number.MAX_SAFE_INTEGER`?** A.

BigInt

B. Float

C. Double

D. Long

Answer: A

Explanation: `BigInt` allows for integers of arbitrary length in JavaScript.

8. **Which is a valid boolean value in JavaScript?**

A. `"true"`

B. `True`

C. `false`

D. `0`

Answer: C

Explanation: JavaScript booleans are lowercase `true` and `false`. The string `"true"` is not a boolean.

9. **Which of these will log `"string"` to the console?**

console.log(typeof __);

A. `typeof 42`

B. `typeof "hello"`

C. `typeof true`

D. `typeof null`

Answer: B

Explanation: `"hello"` is a string literal.

10. **What will `typeof undefinedVar;` return if `undefinedVar` is not declared or assigned?**

A. `"undefined"`

B. `"object"`

C. `"string"`

D. Throws an error

Answer: A

Explanation: An uninitialized variable is `undefined`, and `typeof undefined` is `"undefined"`.

11. **Which of the following is a string concatenation operation in JavaScript?** A. `"Hello" + "World"`

B. `Hello plus World`

C. `concat("Hello", "World")`

D. `"Hello" - "World"`

Answer: A

Explanation: The `+` operator on two string operands concatenates them.

12. **Which of the following is considered falsey in JavaScript?**

A. `true`

B. `"false"`

C. `0`

D. `"0"`

Answer: C

Explanation: `0` is a falsey value, while `"0"` is a truthy string.

13. **What is the type of `Infinity` in JavaScript?**

A. `"number"`

B. `"infinity"`

C. `"bigint"`

D. `"object"`

Answer: A

Explanation: `Infinity` is a numeric value and has type `"number"`.

14. `typeof NaN` returns what value?

A. `"NaN"`

B. `"number"`

C. `"undefined"`

D. `"object"`

Answer: B

Explanation: Even though it stands for "Not a Number," `NaN` is of type `number`.

15. **Which keyword is used to explicitly define an empty or non-existent value?** A. `undefined`

B. `null`

C. `NaN`

D. `void`

Answer: B

Explanation: `null` is the explicit keyword for "no value."

16. **What is the result of `typeof Symbol("id")`?**

A. `"symbol"`

B. `"string"`

C. `"object"`

D. `"function"`

Answer: A

Explanation: Symbols are a distinct primitive type in JavaScript.

17. **Which statement is true about `undefined` vs. `null`?**

A. They are strictly equal.

B. `null` is for declared but uninitialized variables, `undefined` is used for explicit no value. C. `undefined` is for declared but uninitialized variables, `null` is used for explicit no value. D. Both always coerce to an empty string.

Answer: C

Explanation: `undefined` typically means a variable has been declared but not assigned, whereas `null` is an assigned "no value."

18. **What does `parseInt("100abc")` return?**

A. `100`

B. `NaN`

C. `"100abc"`

D. `0`

Answer: A

Explanation: `parseInt` parses as many numeric characters as possible from the start of the string.

19. **What happens if you use arithmetic on a string that cannot be converted to a number?** A. The string is concatenated with the number.

B. A runtime error is thrown.

C. The result is `NaN`.

D. The string is ignored.

Answer: C

Explanation: If a string doesn't contain valid numeric data, arithmetic operations produce `NaN`.

20. **Which of the following would be considered truthy in JavaScript?**

A. `""` (empty string)

B. `null`

C. `"false"` (non-empty string)

D. `0`

Answer: C

Explanation: Any non-empty string is truthy, including `"false"`.

21. **What is the correct result of `"2" * "3"`?**

A. `23`

B. `6`

C. `"6"`

D. Throws an error

Answer: B

Explanation: JavaScript attempts to convert the strings to numbers in multiplication, so `"2" * "3"` = `6`.

22. **What does `typeof NaN === "number"` evaluate to?**

A. `true`

B. `false`

C. `NaN`

D. Throws an error

Answer: A

Explanation: Despite its name, `NaN` is indeed of type `"number"`.

23. **Which of the following is a valid BigInt literal?**

A. `123n`

B. `n123`

C. `123.x`

D. `BigInt(123)`

Answer: A

Explanation: `123n` is the correct literal syntax for a BigInt.

24. **What will `Boolean("0")` return?**

A. `false`

B. `true`

C. `0`

D. `null`

Answer: B

Explanation: Any non-empty string evaluates to `true` when converted to boolean.

25. **What is the result of `typeof (null + 1)`?**

A. `"number"`

B. `"object"`

C. `"undefined"`

D. `"boolean"`

Answer: A

Explanation: `null` in numeric context is `0`, so `null + 1` is `1`, and `typeof 1` is `"number"`.

JavaScript Basic Operators (Arithmetic, Comparison, Logical)

Introduction

Arithmetic Operators

1. `+` (Addition)

2. `-` (Subtraction)

3. `*` (Multiplication)

4. `/` (Division)

5. `%` (Modulo)

6. `**` (Exponentiation in ES7+)

let sum = 5 + 2; // 7

let product = 5 * 2; // 10

let remainder = 5 % 2; // 1

let power = 3 ** 2; // 9

Comparison Operators

1. `>` (Greater than)

2. `<` (Less than)

3. `>=` (Greater than or equal)

4. `<=` (Less than or equal)

5. `==` (Equal to, type-coerced)

6. `!=` (Not equal to, type-coerced)

7. `===` (Strict equality, no type conversion)

8. `!==` (Strict inequality, no type conversion)

console.log(5 == "5"); // true (type coercion)

console.log(5 === "5"); // false (strict comparison)

console.log(10 !== 10); // false

console.log(4 >= 2); // true

Logical Operators

1. `&&` (Logical AND)

2. `||` (Logical OR)

3. `!` (Logical NOT)

let val = (5 > 2) && (2 < 10); // true

val = (5 > 7) || (3 < 4); // true

val = !(5 > 2); // false

Additional Operators

Assignment: `=`, `+=`, `-=`, `*=`, `/=`, `%=`, `**=`

String concatenation with `+` or template literals with backticks.

25 Multiple-Choice Questions: Basic Operators

1. Which operator is used for exponentiation in modern JavaScript?

A. `^`

B. `pow()`

C. `**`

D. `exp()`

Answer: C

Explanation: The `**` operator (introduced in ES7) is used for exponentiation.

2. What is the result of `5 + "10"`?

A. `15`

B. `510`

C. `NaN`

D. Throws an error

Answer: B

Explanation: The `+` operator with a string operand concatenates, resulting in `"510"`. 3.

Which operator is used to check for strict equality without type coercion? A. `==`

B. `===`

C. `=`

D. `!==`

Answer: B

Explanation: `===` checks for equality of value and type.

4. **Which of these is NOT a comparison operator?**

A. `==`

B. `>`

C. `!=`

D. `=`

Answer: D

Explanation: `=` is the assignment operator, not a comparison operator.

5. **What is the result of `10 % 4`?**

A. `2`

B. `4`

C. `6`

D. `0`

Answer: A

Explanation: `10 % 4` is the remainder after dividing 10 by 4, which is 2.

6. Which of the following statements is true about the `&&` operator?

A. Returns the first operand if it is `true`.

B. Returns the second operand if the first operand is truthy.

C. Returns `true` if both operands are truthy; otherwise returns `false`.

D. Always returns a boolean.

Answer: C

Explanation: Logical AND (`&&`) returns `true` only if both operands are truthy.

7. What is the output of `console.log("5" == 5);`?

A. `true`

B. `false`

C. Throws an error

D. `undefined`

Answer: A

Explanation: The `==` operator performs type coercion, so `"5"` == `5` is `true`.

8. Which operator in JavaScript inverts the truth value?

A. `!=`

B. `!!`

C. `? :`

D. `!`

Answer: D

Explanation: `!` is the logical NOT operator, which inverts the boolean value.

9. Which operator can be used for string concatenation if one operand is a string?

A. `+`

B. `-`

C. `*`

D. `%`

Answer: A

Explanation: The `+` operator concatenates if either operand is a string.

10. What will `"5" === 5` evaluate to?

A. `true`

B. `false`

C. `"55"`

D. `"true"`

Answer: B

Explanation: `===` checks both value and type, which do not match here.

11. What is the result of `2 ** 3`?

A. `6`

B. `8`

C. `9`

D. `1`

Answer: B

Explanation: `2 ** 3` is `2` to the power of `3`, which is 8.

12. Which operator checks if operands are NOT strictly equal?

A. `!==`

B. `!=`

C. `=`

D. `==!`

Answer: A

Explanation: `!==` is strict inequality, checking both value and type.

13. What is the result of the expression `(5 > 2) && (2 > 3)`?

A. `true`

B. `false`

C. `undefined`

D. `NaN`

Answer: B

Explanation: `5 > 2` is `true`, but `2 > 3` is `false`. `true && false` is `false`.

14. Which statement about `||` (OR) is correct?

A. Returns true if both operands are true.

B. Returns false if one operand is true.

C. Returns true if at least one operand is truthy.

D. Always returns the first operand.

Answer: C

Explanation: Logical OR (`||`) returns `**true**` if either operand is truthy.

15. **What is `7 % 2`?**

A. `1`

B. `3`

C. `0`

D. `NaN`

Answer: A

Explanation: The remainder of 7 divided by 2 is 1.

16. **Which operator increments the value of a variable by 1?**

A. `--`

B. `+=`

C. `++`

D. `incr`

Answer: C

Explanation: `++` is the increment operator in JavaScript.

17. **What does `a += b` do?**

A. Subtracts `b` from `a`

B. Multiplies `a` by `b`

C. Assigns `a + b` to `a`

D. Assigns `b` to `a`

Answer: C

Explanation: `a += b` is shorthand for `a = a + b`.

18. **How does the `==` operator differ from `===`?**

A. They do not differ at all.

B. `==` checks for reference equality, `===` checks for string equality.

C. `==` coerces types before comparison, `===` does not.

D. `===` is older than `==`.

Answer: C

Explanation: The `==` operator performs type conversion; `===` compares both value and type strictly.

19. **Which of the following comparisons returns `false`?**

A. `5 == "5"`

B. `5 === "5"`

C. `5 != "5"`

D. `5 < 10`

Answer: B

Explanation: `5 === "5"` is false because the types differ.

20. **What is the result of `true && false`?**

A. `true`

B. `false`

C. `undefined`

D. `null`

Answer: B

Explanation: AND returns `false` if either operand is falsey.

21. **What is `typeof (4 + "2")`?**

A. `"string"`

B. `"number"`

C. `NaN`

D. `"undefined"`

Answer: A

Explanation: `"2"` is a string, so `4 + "2"` results in `"42"` which is a string.

22. **Which of the following is the correct exponentiation assignment operator? A. `^=`**

B. `**=`

C. `pow=`

D. `^^=`

Answer: B

Explanation: `**=` is the assignment form of exponentiation in JavaScript.

23. **What is the result of `10 / 0` in JavaScript?**

A. `0`

B. `NaN`

C. `Infinity`

D. Throws an error

Answer: C

Explanation: Division by zero in JavaScript yields `Infinity`.

24. **Which operator checks for equality in value, but not type?**

A. `!==`

B. `==`

C. `===`

D. `=`

Answer: B

Explanation: `==` checks only value after type coercion.

25. **What is the output of `4 > 2 ? "Yes" : "No"`?**

A. `"Yes"`

B. `"No"`

C. `true`

D. `false`

Answer: A

Explanation: The conditional (ternary) operator checks if `4 > 2`. That's `true`, so it returns `"Yes"`.

JavaScript Conditional Statements (if, else, switch) Introduction

In JavaScript, you use

conditional statements to make decisions in your code. `if`

Statement

```
if (condition) {
  // code block executes if condition is truthy
}
```

`if...else` Statement

```
if (condition) {
  // execute if condition is true
} else {
  // execute if condition is false
}
```

`if...else if...else`

```
if (condition1) {
  // code if condition1 is true
} else if (condition2) {
  // code if condition1 is false and condition2 is true
} else {
  // code if all above conditions are false
}
```

`switch` Statement

The `switch` statement evaluates an expression and compares it to multiple `case` clauses: js

```js
switch (expression) {
case value1:
// code block
break;
case value2:
// code block
break;
default:
// code block if no match
}
```

The `break` keyword stops further checks.

`default` executes if no case matches.

Example:

```js
let day = 3;
switch(day) {
case 1:
console.log("Monday");
break;
case 2:
console.log("Tuesday");
break;
case 3:
console.log("Wednesday");
```

```
break;
default:
console.log("Another day");
}
```

25 Multiple-Choice Questions: Conditional Statements

1. Which keyword is used to handle all other cases not matched in a `switch` statement? A. `else`

B. `elif`

C. `default`

D. `otherwise`

Answer: C

Explanation: `default` is executed if no case matches in `switch`.

2. In an `if...else` statement, the `else` block executes when...

A. The condition is true.

B. The condition is false.

C. An error occurs.

D. The condition is always run.

Answer: B

Explanation: The `else` block runs if the `if` condition is falsey.

3. **Which statement can terminate a `case` in a `switch` block?**

A. `end`

B. **`break`**

C. `stop`

D. `return`

Answer: B

Explanation: `break` prevents execution from falling through to subsequent cases.

4. **What will happen if you omit `break` between two `case` blocks?**

A. Throws an error.

B. The code from the next case will execute ("fall-through").

C. The `switch` stops immediately.

D. The `default` case is executed.

Answer: B

Explanation: Without `break`, a switch statement continues execution into the next case.

5. **Which conditional statement allows you to test multiple values efficiently?** A. `if...else`

B. `switch`

C. `ternary`

D. `while`

Answer: B

Explanation: The `switch` statement is often used for checking multiple discrete values.

6. **Which of the following is a valid ternary operator usage?**

A. `if (a < b) ? "Yes" : "No";`

B. `(a < b) ? "Yes" : "No";`

C. `(a < b) if "Yes" else "No";`

D. `switch(a < b) { "Yes": "No"; }`

Answer: B

Explanation: The ternary operator format is `(condition) ? exprIfTrue : exprIfFalse`.

7. **What does an `if` statement require in its parentheses?**

A. A boolean expression

B. A string expression

C. A function call

D. A numeric literal

Answer: A

Explanation: The expression in an `if` statement is evaluated as boolean (truthy/falsy).

8. **What is the purpose of the `else if` clause?**

A. Execute code unconditionally.

B. Check multiple conditions in a sequence.

C. End the `if` statement.

D. It's not a valid JavaScript syntax.

Answer: B

Explanation: `else if` allows chaining multiple conditions.

9. **Which is not a valid conditional structure?**

A. `if (condition) { ... }`

B. `if (condition) { ... } else { ... }`

C. `if (condition) { ... } else if (condition2) { ... }`

D. `when (condition) { ... }`

Answer: D

Explanation: JavaScript does not have a `when` statement for conditionals.

10. **What is the correct syntax of a `switch` statement?**

A.

```
switch {
  case x < 10:
  ...
  default:
  ...
}
```

B.

```
switch(expression) {
  case value: ...
```

default: ...

}

C.

switch(expression) {

 if(value): ...

 else: ...

}

D. `switch{expression -> cases}`

Answer: B

Explanation: That's the correct syntax of a switch statement in JavaScript.

11. **When is the `default` case triggered in a `switch` statement?**

A. Always, regardless of matching cases

B. Only if one of the cases has a matching condition

C. If no case matches

D. If the first case matches

Answer: C

Explanation: `default` is a fallback if no case matches.

12. **Which statement can you use to exit a function inside a `switch` case?**

A. `break`

B. `stop`

C. `exit`

D. `return`

Answer: D

Explanation: `return` exits the function. **break** just exits the switch block.

13. **Which of the following is the correct way to write a simple `if` statement?** A. `if condition: console.log("Hello");`

B. `if (condition) console.log("Hello");`

C. `if [condition] { console.log("Hello"); }`

D. `if {condition} (console.log("Hello"))`

Answer: B

Explanation: Curly braces are optional if only one statement is executed, but parentheses around the condition are mandatory.

14. **Which part of an `if` block is required for it to work?**

A. `if`

B. `else`

C. `else if`

D. `default`

Answer: A

Explanation: Only the `if` part is mandatory. **else** and **else if** are optional.

15. **What is the purpose of `break` in a `switch` statement?**

A. To evaluate the next case

B. To skip the current case

C. To exit the entire switch block

D. To create an error

Answer: C

Explanation: `break` prevents the switch from continuing execution into the next case.

16. **Which operator can act as a one-line `if...else`?**

A. `||`

B. `&&`

C. `?:`

D. `!`

Answer: C

Explanation: The ternary operator `(condition) ? exprIfTrue : exprIfFalse` is a concise one-line `if...else`.

17. **What is the best approach if you have many possible discrete values for a variable?**

A. A large `if...else if` chain

B. A `switch` statement

C. A `while` loop

D. A function call

Answer: B

Explanation: A `switch` statement is typically clearer than multiple `if...else if` statements.

18. **Which line is valid in a `switch` statement?**

A. `case x < 10:`

B. `case "Hello":`

C. `case: 5`

D. `case => 5:`

Answer: B

Explanation: `switch` matches exact values. `case "Hello":` is valid; `case x < 10:` is not used in that manner.

19. **How do you handle multiple identical cases in a switch?**

A. Repeat the `break` statement after each.

B. Duplicate cases are not allowed.

C. You can stack them without a break.

D. You must rewrite them as `if...else if` statements.

Answer: C

Explanation: You can stack cases if they should have the same outcome, as long as you have no `break` in between.

20. **Which is a valid conditional expression for an `if` statement?**

A. `(5 > 2)`

B. `5 > 2;`

C. `var x = (5 > 2);`

D. `function check() { return true; }`

Answer: A

Explanation: The condition must be inside parentheses.
Option B is not inside parentheses, etc.

21. **What will happen if the condition in an `if` statement is always false?** A. The code in the `if` block will never run.

B. The code in the `if` block will run once.

C. It will generate a syntax error.

D. The code after `else` will never run.

Answer: A

Explanation: If the condition is always false, the `if` block's code never executes.

22. **Choose the correct usage of `if...else if...else`:**

A.

if (x > 10) { ... }
if (x > 5) { ... }
else { ... }

B.

if (x > 10) { ... }

else if (x > 5) { ... }

else { ... }

C.

if (x > 10) { ... }

else (x > 5) { ... }

else { ... }

D.

if (x > 10) { ... }

else if x > 5 { ... }

else { ... }

Answer: B

Explanation: `if (condition) { ... } else if

(condition2) { ... } else { ... }` is correct syntax.

23. **Which of the following is required to evaluate a `switch` expression?**

A. A function call

B. A loop

C. A comparison operator

D. A value (expression) that will be matched with cases

Answer: D

Explanation: `switch` uses the expression's resulting value to match against **`case`** labels.

24. **Which code snippet correctly uses a `switch` statement to log `"One"` when `x === 1`? A.**

```
switch (x === 1) {
 case true: console.log("One");
}
```
B.
```
switch (x) {
 case 1: console.log("One");
}
```
C.
```
switch (x) {
 case x === 1: console.log("One");
}
```
D.
```
switch {
 case x = 1: console.log("One");
}
```

Answer: B

Explanation: The switch statement should match `x` to the value `1`.

25. **Which statement about `if...else` is correct?**

A. `else` is mandatory.

B. You can chain multiple `else if` clauses.

C. You cannot have an `if` without an `else`.

D. `if...else` blocks must be inside a function.

Answer: B

Explanation: You can chain several `else if` conditions for sequential checks.

JavaScript Loops (for, while, do...while)

Introduction

Loops allow you to execute a block of code multiple times.

`for` Loop

Syntax:

```
for (initialization; condition; finalExpression) {
// code block
}
```

Example:

```
for (let i = 0; i < 5; i++) {
  console.log(i);
}
```

`while` Loop

Syntax:

```
while (condition) {
// code block
}
```

Example:

```
let j = 0;
while (j < 5) {
  console.log(j);
```

j++;

}

`do...while` Loop

Syntax:

```
do {
 // code block
} while (condition);
```

Example:

```
let k = 0;
do {
 console.log(k);
 k++;
} while (k < 5);
```

A `do...while` loop executes its block at least once before checking the condition.

Breaking and Continuing

`break`: Exits the loop immediately.

`continue`: Skips the current iteration and continues to the next iteration.

25 Multiple-Choice Questions: Loops

1. **Which of the following loops guarantees at least one execution of its body?** A. `for` loop

B. `while` loop

C. `do...while` loop

D. All of the above

Answer: C

Explanation: The `do...while` loop executes its block before checking the condition.

2. **Which loop statement is typically used when you know the exact number of iterations?** A. `for`

B. `while`

C. `do...while`

D. `switch`

Answer: A

Explanation: A `for` loop is ideal when the iteration count is known.

3. **Which statement immediately terminates a loop?**

A. `break`

B. `continue`

C. `exit`

D. `stop`

Answer: A

Explanation: `break` ends the loop immediately.

4. **Which loop checks the condition before executing the loop body?**

A. `while`

B. `do...while`

C. Both `while` and `for`

D. All loops check after execution

Answer: C

Explanation: Both `while` and `for` loops check conditions before running their body.

5. What does `continue` do in a loop?

A. Ends the loop.

B. Skips the current iteration and moves to the next one.

C. Restarts the entire loop.

D. Halts execution with an error.

Answer: B

Explanation: `continue` jumps to the next iteration, skipping the remaining statements in the current loop iteration.

6. What is the correct order of expressions in a `for` loop header?

A. `(condition; initialization; finalExpression)`

B. `(initialization; finalExpression; condition)`

C. `(initialization; condition; finalExpression)`

D. `(finalExpression; condition; initialization)`

Answer: C

Explanation: The standard `for` loop syntax is

`(initialization; condition; finalExpression)`.

7. **Which will log numbers 0 through 4?**

A.

```
for (let i = 0; i <= 5; i++) {
  console.log(i);
}
```

B.

```
for (let i = 0; i < 5; i++) {
  console.log(i);
}
```

C.

```
for (let i = 5; i < 10; i++) {
  console.log(i);
}
```

D.

```
while (0) {
  console.log(i);
}
```

Answer: B

Explanation: `i < 5` will print 0, 1, 2, 3, 4.

8. **Which statement is true about this loop?**

```
let n = 10;
while (n > 0) {
  n--;
```

}

A. It counts `n` from 10 down to 1, then stops when `n` is 0.

B. It's an infinite loop.

C. It never executes.

D. It will produce an error.

Answer: A

Explanation: The loop decrements `n` each time until `n > 0` is false (when `n` is 0).

9. **Which of the following creates an infinite loop?**

A.

```
for (let i = 0; i < 5; i++) {
 console.log(i);
}
```

B.

```
while (true) {
 // ...
}
```

C.

```
do {
 // ...
} while (k < 5);
```

D.

```
for (let i = 0; i <= 10; i++) {
```

```
console.log(i);
}
```

Answer: B

Explanation: `while (true)` runs forever unless a `break` or other exit is used. 10. **Which loop might be preferable to ensure the body runs once before the condition is checked?**

A. `for`

B. `while`

C. `do...while`

D. `if...else`

Answer: C

Explanation: `do...while` executes the body at least once.

11. **How can you exit a loop from inside the loop body?**

A. `break;`

B. `continue;`

C. `return;`

D. No way to exit a loop in JavaScript

Answer: A

Explanation: `break` immediately stops the loop.

12. **In a `while` loop, if the condition is initially false, the loop body will execute...** A. Once

B. Twice

C. Until a `break` statement

D. Not at all

Answer: D

Explanation: If the condition is false from the start, a `while` loop never runs.

13. **Which keyword allows you to skip the current iteration and continue with the next iteration in a loop?**

A. `break`

B. `continue`

C. `skip`

D. `pass`

Answer: B

Explanation: `continue` moves control to the next loop iteration.

14. **Which of the following is a valid `for` loop declaration?**

A.

```
for let i = 0; i < 5; i++ {
  console.log(i);
}
```

B.

```
for (let i; i < 5; i++) {
```

```
console.log(i);
}
```

C.
```
for (let i = 0, i < 5, i++) {
console.log(i);
}
```

D.
```
for (let i = 0; i < 5; i++) {
console.log(i);
}
```

Answer: D

Explanation: The correct syntax is `for (initialization; condition; finalExpression) { ... }`.

15. How do you create an infinite `for` loop?

A. By making the condition always true or never updating the loop variable.

B. `for (let i = 0; i < 0; i++)`

C. Use the `break` statement.

D. JavaScript does not allow infinite loops.

Answer: A

Explanation: If the condition never becomes false or the loop variable never updates, the loop will never end.

16. What will be the output?

```
for (let i = 1; i <= 3; i++) {
```

```
console.log(i);
if (i === 2) break;
}
```

A. `1 2 3`

B. `1 2`

C. `1 3`

D. No output

Answer: B

Explanation: The loop breaks when `i` is `2`, so it prints `1` and `2`.

17. **Which loop increments the counter by 1 on each iteration in this snippet?** js

```
let i = 0;
??? (i < 5) {
 console.log(i);
 i++;
}
```

A. `for`

B. `while`

C. `do...while`

D. All of the above

Answer: B

Explanation: A `while (i < 5)` with `i++` inside will increment by 1 each iteration until `i < 5` is false.

18. **Which keyword is typically used to stop a `while(true)` loop?**

A. `exit`

B. `break`

C. `continue`

D. `stop`

Answer: B

Explanation: `break` is used to exit the loop.

19. **What is the main difference between a `while` loop and a `do...while` loop?** A. `while` always runs at least once, `do...while` may not run at all.

B. `while` checks the condition after each iteration, `do...while` checks before. C. `do...while` executes the loop body at least once, `while` may execute zero times. D. There is no difference.

Answer: C

Explanation: `do...while` performs at least one iteration before checking its condition.

20. **Which of the following is NOT a loop in JavaScript?**

A. `for`

B. `while`

C. `foreach`

D. `do...while`

Answer: C

Explanation: Although `forEach` exists as an array method, it is not a standalone JavaScript statement like `for`, `while`, or `do...while`.

21. **What happens if the loop variable in a `for` loop is never updated inside the loop body?** A. It becomes `undefined`.

B. It executes only once.

C. It will cause an infinite loop if the condition depends on it.

D. No effect on the loop.

Answer: C

Explanation: If the condition never changes, the loop will not end (unless the condition is initially false).

22. **Which loop structure is typically used when the exact number of iterations is unknown?** A. `for` loop

B. `while` loop

C. `for...of` loop

D. `for...in` loop

Answer: B

Explanation: A `while` loop is often used when we don't know how many times we'll iterate.

23. **What is the effect of using `continue` in a `do...while` loop?**

A. It re-initializes the variable.

B. It ends the loop.

C. It skips the rest of the current iteration and checks the condition again.

D. It restarts the entire loop from the beginning.

Answer: C

Explanation: `continue` moves on to the next iteration by re-checking the condition.

24. **Which is the correct loop to sum numbers from 1 to 5?**

A.

```
let sum = 0;
for (let i = 1; i <= 5; i++) {
 sum += i;
}
```

B.

```
let sum = 0;
while (i <= 5) {
 sum += i;
}
```

C.

```
let sum = 0;
for (let i = 1; i < 5; i++) {
 sum += i;
}
```

D.

```
let sum = 0;
while (sum < 5) {
 sum++;
}
```

Answer: A

Explanation: `(let i = 1; i <= 5; i++)` accumulates `1 + 2 + 3 + 4 + 5` into `sum`. 25. **Which loop runs as long as `i < 5`, checking the condition prior to each iteration, and increments `i` within the loop body?**

A.

```
do {
 console.log(i);
 i++;
} while (i < 5);
```

B.

```
for (let i = 0; i < 5; i++) {
```

```
console.log(i);
}
```
C.
```
while (i < 5) {
console.log(i);
 i++;
}
```
D.
```
switch (i < 5) {
 case true: i++;
}
```
Answer: C

Explanation: A `while (i < 5)` checks `i < 5` before each iteration and increments `i` inside the block.

JavaScript Basic Functions (Function Declaration and Invocation)

Introduction

Functions are reusable blocks of code. You can define a function with the **function declaration** or **function expression**, and invoke (call) it to execute its body.

Function Declaration

```
function greet() {
console.log("Hello!");
```

```
}
greet(); // invocation
```

You can also pass **parameters** to functions:

```
function add(a, b) {
 return a + b;
}
console.log(add(2, 3)); // 5
```

Function Expression

```
const sayHello = function(name) {
 return "Hello, " + name;
};
console.log(sayHello("Alice"));
```

Arrow Functions (ES6+)

```
const multiply = (x, y) => x * y;
console.log(multiply(3, 4)); // 12
```

Return Statement

The `return` keyword ends function execution and returns the specified value. If no `return` is specified, the function returns `undefined`.

25 Multiple-Choice Questions: Basic Functions

1. **How do you declare a function named `myFunc` in JavaScript?**

A. `function = myFunc() { ... }`

B. `function myFunc() { ... }`

C. `declare function myFunc() { ... }`

D. `func myFunc { ... }`

Answer: B

Explanation: The standard function declaration syntax is `function myFunc() { ... }`.

2. What is the default return value of a function that doesn't explicitly `return`? A. `null`

B. `undefined`

C. `0`

D. `""`

Answer: B

Explanation: If no value is returned, the function returns `undefined`.

3. Which keyword ends the execution of a function and specifies its return value? A. `break`

B. `continue`

C. `exit`

D. `return`

Answer: D

Explanation: `return` ends function

execution and specifies the returned value. 4. **What is the correct syntax to call a function named `displayMessage`?**

A. `call displayMessage;`

B. `function displayMessage();`

C. `displayMessage();`

D. `execute(displayMessage);`

Answer: C

Explanation: You invoke a function by writing its name followed by parentheses: `displayMessage()`.

5. **What does the following function return?**

function test() {
 console.log("Hello");
}

A. `"Hello"`

B. `undefined`

C. `null`

D. Throws an error

Answer: B

Explanation: Since there is no `return`, the function returns `undefined`.

6. **How many parameters can a JavaScript function have?**

A. Only 1

B. Only 2

C. 0 to many

D. Exactly 3

Answer: C

Explanation: A JavaScript function can have zero or more parameters.

7. **Which is a valid way to define a function expression?**

A.

```
var myFunc = function() {
 return 5;
};
```

B.

```
function expression myFunc {
 return 5;
}
```

C.

```
expression myFunc() {
 return 5;
}
```

D.

```
var myFunc => function() {
```

```
return 5;
};
```

Answer: A

Explanation: A function expression is assigned to a variable, e.g. `var myFunc = function() { ... };`.

8. Which arrow function correctly multiplies two numbers?

A. `const multiply = (x, y) => { return x * y };`

B. `const multiply = x, y => x * y;`

C. `arrow multiply(x, y) => x * y;`

D. `const multiply = (x, y) => x, y;`

Answer: A

Explanation: You can optionally omit curly braces if you just return the expression: `(x, y) => x * y`.

9. What is function hoisting?

A. Ability to reuse functions.

B. Moving all function declarations to the top of the file.

C. The technique of calling a function multiple times.

D. Keeping function scope local.

Answer: B

Explanation: Function declarations are hoisted, meaning they're read into memory at compilation.

10. How do you pass an argument to a function with a

parameter `name`?

A. `myFunc.name = "Alex";`

B. `myFunc("Alex");`

C. `myFunc:("Alex");`

D. `name("Alex");`

Answer: B

Explanation: You call `myFunc("Alex")`, passing `"Alex"` to the parameter `name`.

11. **Which of the following is a function declaration rather than a function expression?** A.

```
let greet = function() {
 console.log("Hello");
};
```

B.

```
function greet() {
 console.log("Hello");
}
```

C.

```
const greet = () => {
 console.log("Hello");
};
```

D.

```
var greet = function() {
```

```
    console.log("Hello");
};
```

Answer: B

Explanation: `function greet() { ... }` is a declaration; the others are expressions. 12. **Which statement is true about an arrow function with no parameters? A.** `const myFunc = => { ... }` is valid.

B. `const myFunc = () => { ... }` is valid.

C. `const myFunc = [] => { ... }` is valid.

D. `const myFunc = (params) => { ... }` is required.

Answer: B

Explanation: If an arrow function has no parameters, you use empty parentheses `()`.

13. **Which part of the function definition is used to specify its name?**

A. The parentheses

B. The curly braces

C. The function identifier before parentheses

D. The return statement

Answer: C

Explanation: The function name is specified before the parentheses in a function declaration, e.g. `function` name() { ... }`.

14. **Which function does not explicitly return a value, so it returns `undefined`?** A.

function greet() {

 return "Hi!";

}

B.

function sum(a, b) {

 return a + b;

}

C.

function logger() {

 console.log("Log something");

}

D.

function multiply(x, y) {

 return x * y;

}

Answer: C

Explanation: The `logger` function only logs to the console; it doesn't have a `return` statement.

15. **Which syntax is used to define a function with a block body in arrow**

functions? A. `() -> { ... }`

B. `() => { ... }`

C. `[] => { ... }`

D. `func => { ... }`

Answer: B

Explanation: The correct arrow function syntax with a block body is `() => { ... }`. 16. **What will `sum(5, 10)` return given the code below?**

```
function sum(a, b) {
 console.log(a + b);
}
```

A. `15`

B. `undefined`

C. `NaN`

D. It throws an error

Answer: B

Explanation: The function logs `15` to the console but doesn't return anything, so the result is `undefined`.

17. **Which is the correct way to write a function that returns the square of a number in arrow function form?**

A. `const square = x => x * x;`

B. `const square = x => { x * x };`

C. `const square = (x) => { return x x; };`

D. `const square => (x) => x * x;`

Answer: A

Explanation: `(x) => x * x` is a concise arrow function returning `x * x`.

18. **Where does the function name appear in a function expression?**

A. Before the parentheses.

B. It doesn't need a name; it can be anonymous if assigned to a variable.

C. After the parentheses, inside curly braces.

D. JavaScript doesn't allow function expressions.

Answer: B

Explanation: Function expressions can be anonymous, e.g. `const foo = function() { ... };`.

19. **Which of the following statements is true about arrow functions and `this` keyword?** A. They have their own `this`.

B. They use the `this` of the enclosing lexical scope.

C. They create a new `this` context each time they are invoked.

D. They remove the need for `this`.

Answer: B

Explanation: Arrow functions inherit `this` from their surrounding context.

20. **What happens if you call a function with fewer arguments than parameters?** A. The missing parameters are `undefined`

B. Throws a `ReferenceError`

C. The function returns `null`

D. The extra parameters are automatically set to 0

Answer: A

Explanation: Missing arguments result in `undefined` parameters in the function body.

21. **Which statement is true about function declarations vs function expressions?** A. Function declarations are hoisted, function expressions are not fully hoisted with initial value. B. Both are not hoisted. C. Only function expressions are hoisted.

D. Neither is valid in modern JavaScript.

Answer: A

Explanation: Declarations are hoisted in entirety. Expressions are partially hoisted (the variable name is hoisted, but not its assignment).

22. **Which function syntax is valid in JavaScript?**

A. `function :foo() { ... }`

B. `const foo = function bar() { ... };`

C. `function = foo() { ... }`

D. `func foo { ... }`

Answer: B

Explanation: Named function expressions are valid, e.g.

`const foo = function bar() { ... };`.

23. **Which is the correct statement about a function with no parameters?**

A. It must include parentheses `()`.

B. It can't return a value.

C. It must have at least one parameter.

D. It's invalid syntax.

Answer: A

Explanation: Even with no parameters, you must have empty parentheses to define a function.

24. **Which is a self-invoking function pattern (IIFE)?**

A.

```
function() {
 console.log("Hello");
}();
```

B.

```
(function() {
 console.log("Hello");
```

})();

C.

```
function iife() {
 console.log("Hello");
}
iife();
```

D.

```
(() => { console.log("Hello"); });
```

Answer: B

Explanation: `(function() { ... })();` is the classic Immediately Invoked Function Expression pattern.

25. **What is the result of this code?**

```
function foo() {
 return
 {
 bar: 10
 };
}
console.log(foo());
```

A. `{ bar: 10 }`

B. `undefined`

C. `null`

D. Throws an error

Answer: B

Explanation: Due to automatic semicolon insertion, `return` ends the statement. The object is never returned; the function returns `undefined`.

Working with the DOM

Selecting Elements (getElementById, querySelector, etc.) Introduction

In JavaScript, interacting with the web page (the DOM) often starts with **selecting elements**. The DOM (Document Object Model) represents the HTML document as a tree structure, allowing us to programmatically access, modify, or create new elements.

Common Methods of Selecting Elements

1. `document.getElementById("id")`

Selects the element with a matching `id` attribute.

Returns a single `HTMLElement` or `null` if not found.

```
<!-- Example HTML -->
<div id="main-container">Hello World</div>
const container = document.getElementById("main-container");
console.log(container); // <div id="main-container">Hello World</div>
```

2. `document.getElementsByClassName("className")`

Selects all elements that have a specific class.

Returns an **HTMLCollection**, which is a live collection of elements.

```
<p class="description">Paragraph 1</p>
<p class="description">Paragraph 2</p>
const paragraphs =
document.getElementsByClassName("description");
console.log(paragraphs[0]); // <p
class="description">Paragraph 1</p>
```

3. `document.getElementsByTagName("tagName")`

Selects all elements with a specified tag name.

Returns an **HTMLCollection**.

```
const listItems = document.getElementsByTagName("li");
```

4. `document.querySelector("selector")`

Selects the **first** element that matches a CSS selector.

Returns a single `Element` or `null` if no match is found.

```
const firstParagraph =
document.querySelector(".description");
```

5. `document.querySelectorAll("selector")`

Selects **all** elements that match a CSS selector.

Returns a **NodeList**, which can be iterated over like an array (although not all array methods work).

```
const allParagraphs =
```

```
document.querySelectorAll(".description");
```

Differences Between HTMLCollection and NodeList

HTMLCollection:

Live collection (updates automatically when DOM changes).

Returned by `getElementsByClassName` and `getElementsByTagName`.

NodeList:

Static collection (usually, except for cases like `childNodes`).

Returned by `querySelectorAll`.

Practical Code Examples

```html
<!DOCTYPE html>
<html>
<head>
 <title>DOM Selection Example</title>
</head>
<body>
 <div id="main">
 <p class="text">Paragraph 1</p>
 <p class="text">Paragraph 2</p>
 <span>Span Text</span>
 </div>
 <script>
 // By ID
```

```javascript
const mainDiv = document.getElementById("main");
console.log(mainDiv);
// By class name
const textParas =
document.getElementsByClassName("text");
console.log(textParas[0]);
// By tag name
const spans = document.getElementsByTagName("span");
console.log(spans[0]);
// Using querySelector
const firstTextPara = document.querySelector(".text");
console.log(firstTextPara);
// Using querySelectorAll
const allTextParas = document.querySelectorAll(".text");
allTextParas.forEach(para => {
console.log(para.textContent);
});
</script>
</body>
</html>
```

The above examples demonstrate different ways to select elements and then log them or their properties (`**textContent**`) to the console.

25 Multiple-Choice Questions: Selecting Elements

1. **Which method returns the first matching element for a given CSS selector?** A. `document.querySelectorAll()`

B. `document.getElementById()`

C. `document.querySelector()`

D. `document.getElementsByTagName()`

Answer: C

Explanation: `document.querySelector()` returns the first matching element.

2. **Which method is specifically used to select elements by their `id` attribute?**

A. `document.getElementById()`

B. `document.querySelector("#id")`

C. `document.getElementByClassName()`

D. `document.id()`

Answer: A

Explanation: `document.getElementById("id")` is the standard method for selecting an element by its unique `id`.

3. **Which method returns an HTMLCollection?**

A. `document.querySelectorAll()`

B. `document.getElementsByClassName()`

C. `document.getElementById()`

D. `document.querySelector()`

Answer: B

Explanation: `getElementsByClassName()` and `getElementsByTagName()` return an HTMLCollection.

4. **What does `document.querySelectorAll(".myClass")` return?**

A. A single DOM element

B. A HTMLCollection

C. A NodeList of all elements with the class `myClass`

D. None of the above

Answer: C

Explanation: `querySelectorAll()` returns a NodeList of all matching elements.

5. **Which method is commonly used to select the first `<p>` element in the document?** A. `document.getElementsByName("p")`

B. `document.querySelector("p")`

C. `document.querySelectorAll("p")[1]`

D. `document.getElementById("p")`

Answer: B

Explanation: `document.querySelector("p")` selects the first `<p>` in the document.

6. What is a key difference between an HTMLCollection and a NodeList?

A. NodeList is always live, HTMLCollection is always static.

B. HTMLCollection is always empty.

C. NodeList is typically static, while HTMLCollection is live.

D. There is no difference; they are the same type.

Answer: C

Explanation: `HTMLCollection` is live, `NodeList` is typically static (except certain cases).

7. Which selection method can be used to find elements based on a tag name like `<div>`? A. `document.getElementsByClassName("div")`

B. `document.getElementByTagName("div")`

C. `document.getElementsByTagName("div")`

D. `document.querySelectorAll("#div")`

Answer: C

Explanation: `document.getElementsByTagName("div")` is used to select elements by tag name.

8. Which of the following returns `null` if no element is found?

A. `document.querySelector()`

B. `document.getElementsByClassName()`

C. `document.getElementsByTagName()`

D. `document.querySelectorAll()`

Answer: A

Explanation: `document.querySelector()` returns `null` if no match is found; similarly, `getElementById()` can also return `null`.

9. **Which is the correct syntax to select an element with the id of `main` using query selector?** A. `document.querySelector("main")`

B. `document.querySelector(".main")`

C. `document.querySelector("#main")`

D. `document.querySelector("id='main'")`

Answer: C

Explanation: In CSS syntax, `#main` targets the element whose id is `main`.

10. **What does `document.getElementById("header")` return if there is no element with `id="header"`?**

A. It returns an empty array.

B. It returns an empty string.

C. It throws an error.

D. It returns `null`.

Answer: D

Explanation: `getElementById()` returns `null` if no matching element exists.

11. **Which method will you use to select all elements matching `.info > p` (p tags that are direct children of an element with class `info`)?**

A. `document.querySelector(".info > p")`

B. `document.querySelectorAll(".info > p")`

C. `document.getElementsByTagName("p")`

D. `document.getElementsByClassName("info > p")`

Answer: B

Explanation: `document.querySelectorAll(".info > p")` selects all `<p>` elements that are direct children of `.info`.

12. **Which method returns the first `<div>` inside a container with class `box`?** A. `document.getElementById("box").getElementsByTagName("div")`

B. `document.querySelector(".box div")`

C. `document.querySelectorAll(".box div")[0]`

D. Both B and C are correct ways

Answer: D

Explanation: `querySelector(".box div")` returns the first matching `<div>`. Alternatively, `querySelectorAll(".box div")[0]` returns the first from the NodeList.

13. **Which of the following is a property of the NodeList returned by**
`document.querySelectorAll()`?

A. It doesn't support iteration.

B. It is automatically updated when the DOM changes.

C. It's typically static.

D. It always contains exactly one element.

Answer: C

Explanation: A NodeList from `querySelectorAll()` is usually static, unlike HTMLCollection which is live.

14. **What does `document.querySelectorAll("p.intro")`**
select?

A. All `<p>` elements with class `intro`.

B. All `.intro` elements inside `<p>`.

C. The first `<p>` element with class `intro`.

D. A single NodeList containing `<p>` elements with id `intro`.

Answer: A

Explanation: `p.intro` is a CSS selector meaning "all `<p>` with class `intro`."

15. **What is returned by**
`document.getElementsByClassName("card")` if there

are three elements with that class?

A. An array with three elements

B. A HTMLCollection with three elements

C. A NodeList with three elements

D. A single element

Answer: B

Explanation: `getElementsByClassName("card")` returns a live HTMLCollection.

16. **Which statement is true about `document.querySelector("#myId")`?**

A. It selects an element by class.

B. It selects all elements with `id="myId"`.

C. It selects the first element with `id="myId"`.

D. It always returns an empty NodeList.

Answer: C

Explanation: `#myId` is the CSS syntax for an element with that ID, and `querySelector` returns the first match.

17. **What does `document.getElementsByTagName("ul")` return?**

A. A single `ul` element

B. A HTMLCollection of all `<ul>` elements in the document

C. A NodeList of all `<ul>` elements in the document

D. A single NodeList with only the first `<ul>`

Answer: B

Explanation: `getElementsByTagName()` returns a live HTMLCollection of the matched elements.

18. **Which method can select multiple IDs at once?**

A. `document.getElementById("#id1, #id2")`

B. `document.querySelectorAll("#id1, #id2")`

C. `document.getElementsById("id1, id2")`

D. None of the above

Answer: B

Explanation: `querySelectorAll("#id1, #id2")` can match multiple ID selectors at once (though it's unusual to have multiple items with the same ID in valid HTML).

19. **Which property best describes an HTMLCollection?**

A. It cannot be accessed by index.

B. It is automatically updated if the DOM changes.

C. It is read-only and cannot change.

D. You can call `forEach()` directly on it.

Answer: B

Explanation: An HTMLCollection is live and updates when the DOM changes.

20. **When using `document.querySelectorAll(".item")`, how can you access the second matched element?**

A. `document.querySelectorAll(".item").second`

B. `document.querySelector(".item")[1]`

C. `document.querySelectorAll(".item")[1]`

D. `document.querySelector(".item").secondChild`

Answer: C

Explanation: A NodeList can be accessed by index, so `[1]` gets the second element.

21. **Which statement is true about selecting elements by `document.getElementById("uniqueId")`?** A. It returns an array of elements with **uniqueId**.

B. It returns the first match.

C. It returns exactly one element with that ID.

D. It returns a NodeList of length 1.

Answer: C

Explanation: An ID should be unique in HTML, so `getElementById` returns one element or `null`.

22. **What is the correct way to select all `<li>` elements inside a `<ul class="menu">` using query methods?**

A. `document.querySelectorAll("li .menu")`

B. `document.querySelectorAll("ul.menu li")`

C. `document.querySelector("ul.menu li")`

D. `document.getElementById(".menu li")`

Answer: B

Explanation: `"ul.menu li"` means "all `<li>` elements inside `<ul class="menu">`."

23. **If you only want the first matching**
`.box` **element, which method do you**
use? A.
`document.querySelectorAll(".box")[0]`

B. `document.querySelector(".box")`

C. `document.getElementsByClassName("box")[0]`

D. All of the above are valid ways

Answer: D

Explanation: All three approaches can give you the first
`.box`. `querySelector(".box")` directly returns the first.
`querySelectorAll(".box")[0]` and
`getElementsByClassName("box")[0]` also return the
first item from the collection.

24. **What happens if**
`document.querySelector("div.myClass")` **is called**
and there is no `<div>` **with class** `myClass`?

A. Returns `null`

B. Returns `undefined`

C. Throws a runtime error

D. Returns an empty object

Answer: A

Explanation: `querySelector()` returns `null` if no
elements match.

25. Which method cannot directly accept a CSS selector?

A. `document.querySelector()`

B. `document.getElementById()`

C. `document.querySelectorAll()`

D. None of the above

Answer: B

Explanation: `getElementById()` only takes a string ID, not a full CSS selector.

Changing Element Content and Attributes

Introduction

After selecting elements, you'll often want to modify them—changing their text, HTML content, style, or attributes.

Changing Text Content

`element.textContent`: A property that sets or returns the textual content of an element, stripping HTML tags.

const p = document.querySelector("#myParagraph");

p.textContent = "New text goes here!";

Changing Inner HTML

`element.innerHTML`: A property that gets or sets the HTML content of an element. This can include nested elements and tags.

const container = document.querySelector("#container");

container.innerHTML = "<p>Paragraph inside

container</p>";

Caution: Setting `innerHTML` with user input can lead to security issues like XSS if not handled properly.

Modifying Attributes

1. `element.setAttribute("attrName", "value")`

Sets a specified attribute to a given value.

const link = document.querySelector("a");

link.setAttribute("href", "https://example.com");

2. `element.getAttribute("attrName")`

Retrieves the current value of an attribute.

const currentHref = link.getAttribute("href");

3. `element.removeAttribute("attrName")`

Removes an attribute from an element.

link.removeAttribute("title");

Changing Styles

You can modify an element's style via the `style` property:

const box = document.querySelector(".box");

box.style.backgroundColor = "red";

box.style.width = "200px";

Alternatively, you can toggle, add, or remove classes to change styles:

box.classList.add("highlight");

```
box.classList.remove("hidden");
box.classList.toggle("visible");
```

Practical Code Example

```html
<!DOCTYPE html>
<html>
<head>
 <title>Change Content and Attributes Example</title>
</head>
<body>
 <p id="message">Old text</p>
 <img id="image" src="old.jpg" alt="Old Image">
 <script>
const message = document.getElementById("message");
// Change text
message.textContent = "New text content!";
const image = document.getElementById("image");
// Change attribute
image.setAttribute("src", "new.jpg");
image.setAttribute("alt", "New Image");
// Add some HTML
message.innerHTML += " <strong>with bold
text!</strong>";
 </script>
</body>
```

</html>

25 Multiple-Choice Questions: Changing Element Content and Attributes

1. Which property do you use to change the text within an element without preserving any HTML tags?

A. `innerHTML`

B. `textContent`

C. `innerText`

D. `value`

Answer: B

Explanation: `textContent` changes only the text, ignoring any HTML tags.

2. Which property replaces the entire HTML content of an element?

A. `outerHTML`

B. `innerText`

C. `innerHTML`

D. `value`

Answer: C

Explanation: `innerHTML` sets or gets the HTML content inside an element.

3. How do you set the `href` attribute of a link element

using JavaScript?

A. `link.href = "https://example.com";`

B. `link.setAttribute("href", "https://example.com");`

C. Both A and B can work

D. `link.attribute.href = "example.com";`

Answer: C

Explanation: You can directly set the `href` property, or use `setAttribute()`.

4. **What is a potential security concern when setting `innerHTML`?**

A. Overwriting CSS classes

B. Memory leaks

C. XSS (Cross-Site Scripting) if user input is inserted unsafely

D. Performance overhead

Answer: C

Explanation: `innerHTML` can introduce XSS vulnerabilities if untrusted user input is used.

5. **Which is the best method to retrieve the `src` attribute from an `<img>` element?** A. `img.getAttribute("src")`

B. `img.src`

C. Both A and B will get the current source

D. `img.innerHTML`

Answer: C

Explanation: You can use either `getAttribute("src")` or `img.src`.

6. **Which property directly modifies an element's inline style in JavaScript?** A. `element.inlineStyle`

B. `element.style`

C. `element.css`

D. `element.property`

Answer: B

Explanation: The `style` property is used for inline styles in JavaScript.

7. **How would you remove the `alt` attribute from an `<img>` element?**

A. `img.alt = "";`

B. `img.remove("alt");`

C. `img.removeAttribute("alt");`

D. `img.removeAlt();`

Answer: C

Explanation: `element.removeAttribute("attrName")` removes an attribute.

8. **Which statement is true about `textContent` vs.**

`innerHTML`?

A. `textContent` and `innerHTML` always return the same string.

B. `textContent` preserves HTML tags; `innerHTML` does not.

C. `innerHTML` can contain HTML markup, `textContent` shows only text.

D. Both are deprecated in modern JavaScript.

Answer: C

Explanation: `innerHTML` renders HTML tags, whereas `textContent` returns only text.

9. **Which method is used to add a CSS class to an element?**

A. `element.class = "classname";`

B. `element.classList.add("classname");`

C. `element.setAttribute("className", "classname");`

D. `element.addClass("classname");`

Answer: B

Explanation: `classList.add("classname")` is the standard way to add a class in modern JavaScript.

10. **How can you set a `title` attribute on a `<p>` element?**

A. `paragraph.setAttribute("title", "MyTitle");`

B. `paragraph.title("MyTitle");`

C. `paragraph.getAttribute("title", "MyTitle");`

D. `paragraph.classList.title = "MyTitle";`

Answer: A

Explanation: `setAttribute("title", "MyTitle")` sets the `title` attribute.

11. **If you want to append a bold text `<strong>Hi</strong>` at the end of an element's existing HTML, which approach is correct?**

A. `element.textContent += "<strong>Hi</strong>";`

B. `element.innerHTML += "<strong>Hi</strong>";`

C. `element.appendChild("<strong>Hi</strong>");`

D. `element.addHTML("<strong>Hi</strong>");`

Answer: B

Explanation: `element.innerHTML += ...` appends HTML to existing content.

12. **Which function would you call to remove a `disabled` attribute from a button?** A. `button.removeDisabled();`

B. `button.setAttribute("disabled", false);`

C. `button.removeAttribute("disabled");`

D. `button.disabled = true;`

Answer: C

Explanation: Removing an attribute is done via

`removeAttribute()`.

13. What will happen if you set `element.innerHTML` to an empty string?

A. It clears all child elements within **`element`**.

B. It removes the **`element`** from the DOM.

C. It throws an error.

D. It does nothing.

Answer: A

Explanation: Setting `innerHTML = ""` removes all contents inside that element.

14. How would you change the background color of an element with an ID of `box` to `blue` using inline style?

A.
`document.getElementById("box").se tAttribute("background-color", "blue");` B.
`document.getElementById("box").bg color = "blue";`

C.
`document.getElementById("box").style.backgroundCol or = "blue";`

D. `document.getElementById("box").color = "blue";`

Answer: C

Explanation: `element.style.backgroundColor` is the

correct property for setting the inline style.

15. **Which of the following correctly changes the alt text of an `<img>` element?** A. `img.setAttribute("alt", "New alt text");`

B. `img.alt = "New alt text";`

C. Both A and B

D. `img.innerHTML = "New alt text";`

Answer: C

Explanation: You can either use `setAttribute("alt", ...)` or directly set `img.alt = "...";`.

16. **Which method can directly remove all child nodes of a selected element?** A. `element.innerHTML = "";`

B. `element.removeAllChildren();`

C. `element.childNodes = [];`

D. None of the above

Answer: A

Explanation: Setting `innerHTML` to an empty string effectively removes all child nodes. 17. **How can you add multiple classes (`"highlight"` and `"big"`) to an element at once using `classList`?**

A. `element.classList.add("highlight", "big");`

B. `element.classList.add(["highlight", "big"]);`

C. `element.setAttribute("class", "highlight big");`

D. `element.className += " highlight big";`

Answer: A

Explanation: Modern browsers allow
`classList.add("highlight", "big")` with
multiple arguments.

18. **Which property would you use to read the computed style of an element in JavaScript? A. `element.style`**

B. `element.currentStyle`

C. `window.getComputedStyle(element)`

D. `element.computedStyle`

Answer: C

Explanation: `window.getComputedStyle(element)` is
used to get the final computed style from CSS.

19. **Which method would append `<div>New Content</div>` to an element's current HTML content?**

A. `element.innerHTML = "<div>New Content</div>";`

B. `element.innerHTML += "<div>New Content</div>";`

C. `element.textContent += "<div>New Content</div>";`

D. `element.appendChild("<div>New Content</div>");`

Answer: B

Explanation: Using `+=` appends HTML to existing `innerHTML`.

20. **If you want to add an attribute `data-value="10"` to a `<div>`, which is valid? A. `div.setAttribute("data-value", "10");`**

B. `div.dataValue = "10";`

C. `div.attribute("data-value") = 10;`

D. `div.value = "10";`

Answer: A

Explanation: `setAttribute()` sets the attribute properly, e.g., `div.setAttribute("data-value", "10")`.

21. **Which property indicates or changes the entire outer HTML, including the element itself? A. `element.innerHTML`**

B. `element.textContent`

C. `element.outerHTML`

D. `element.htmlContent`

Answer: C

Explanation: `outerHTML` includes the element itself and its content.

22. **How do you remove the content but keep the element in the DOM?**

A. `element.parentNode.removeChild(element);`

B. `element.innerHTML = "";`

C. `element.remove();`

D. `element.outerHTML = "";`

Answer: B

Explanation: `element.innerHTML = ""` empties the element's content without removing the element itself.

23. **Which approach is correct to *directly* set multiple inline styles at once?**

A. `element.style = "color: red; background: blue;";`

B. `element.setAttribute("style", "color: red; background: blue;");`

C. Both A and B

D. `element.cssStyle = { color: "red", background: "blue" };`

Answer: C

Explanation: You can use either `element.style = "..."` or `element.setAttribute("style", "...")`. Usually, though, setting `element.style.propertyName` is safer and more granular.

24. **Which is the best method to *safely* insert dynamic text into an element?**

A. `element.innerHTML = userInput;`

B. `element.textContent = userInput;`

C. `element.html = userInput;`

D. `element.innerHTML += userInput;`

Answer: B

Explanation: `textContent` escapes any HTML and thus avoids XSS vulnerabilities if the input is untrusted.

25. **Which property would you change to rename a class from ``title`` to ``main-title``?** A. `element.className = "main-title";`

B. `element.class = "main-title";`

C. `element.classListName = "main-title";`

D. `element.renameClass("title", "main-title");`

Answer: A

Explanation: Setting `element.className` to a new string replaces all existing classes with the new one.

Event Listeners and Event Handling

Introduction

Events let you respond to user actions (clicks, key presses, etc.) or system events (page load, etc.). In JavaScript, you can attach **event listeners** to HTML elements so that when an event fires, a function (the event handler) is called.

Adding Event Listeners

`element.addEventListener("eventType", callbackFunction)`

Attaches an event listener to `element`. Common events:
`"click"`, `"mouseover"`, `"keyup"`, etc. const button =
document.querySelector("#myButton");

```
button.addEventListener("click", function() {
  console.log("Button clicked!");
});
```

Removing Event Listeners:

To remove, you must have a reference to the exact function
used:

```
function handleClick() {
  console.log("Button clicked!");
}
button.addEventListener("click", handleClick);
// Later
button.removeEventListener("click", handleClick);
```

Event Object

When an event is triggered, a special **event object** is
passed to the handler, containing details like `target`
(the element that triggered the event), mouse
coordinates, key pressed, etc.

```
button.addEventListener("click", function(event) {
  console.log("Event target:", event.target);
});
```

Common Event Types

Mouse Events: `click`, `dblclick`, `mousedown`, `mouseup`, `mouseover`, `mouseout`, etc. **Keyboard Events:** `keydown`, `keyup`, `keypress`.

Form Events: `submit`, `change`, `focus`, `blur`.

Window Events: `load`, `resize`, `scroll`, etc.

Inline Event Handlers (Not Recommended)

You can also add events directly in HTML, e.g., `<button onclick="myFunc()">Click</button>`, but this is generally less flexible and considered outdated in favor of the modern `addEventListener`.

Preventing Default Behavior

Some events have default actions (e.g., clicking a link navigates to another page). You can prevent this with:

```
link.addEventListener("click", function(e) {
 e.preventDefault();
});
```

Stopping Propagation

Event bubbling is when an event travels up the DOM tree. You can stop further propagation with: js e.stopPropagation();

Practical Code Example

```
<!DOCTYPE html>
```

```
<html>
<head>
 <title>Event Listener Example</title>
</head>
<body>
 <button id="clickMe">Click Me</button>
 <a href="https://example.com" id="myLink">Go to
Example.com</a>
 <script>
 const btn = document.getElementById("clickMe");
 btn.addEventListener("click", function(event) {
 alert("Button was clicked!");
 console.log("Event type:", event.type);
 });
 const link = document.getElementById("myLink");
 link.addEventListener("click", function(e) {
 e.preventDefault(); // Prevent navigation
 console.log("Link click prevented!");
 });
 </script>
</body>
</html>
```

25 Multiple-Choice Questions: Event Listeners and Event Handling

1. **Which method is used to attach an event listener to an element in modern JavaScript?** A. `element.onEvent()`

B. `element.setListener()`

C. `element.addEventListener()`

D. `element.attachEvent()`

Answer: C

Explanation: `addEventListener()` is the standard way to attach event listeners. 2. **Which event is triggered when a user clicks on an element?**

A. `click`

B. `mousedown`

C. `keyup`

D. `mouseover`

Answer: A

Explanation: The `click` event fires when the user clicks an element.

3. **How do you remove an event listener that was previously added with `addEventListener`?** A. `element.removeEventListener("eventType", function() {});`

B. `element.clearEventListener("eventType");`

C. `element.eventType = null;`

D. `element.deleteListener("eventType", callback);`

Answer: A

Explanation: `removeEventListener("eventType", callbackFunction)` is used to remove an event listener.

4. **What is passed to the callback function when an event is triggered?**

A. The DOM element itself

B. The event object (`event`)

C. A boolean indicating success or failure

D. Nothing

Answer: B

Explanation: The event object, containing details about the event, is passed to the callback.

5. **Which is a valid way to define a click handler for a button with an ID `myBtn`?** A.

myBtn.onclick = function() {
 console.log("Clicked!");
};

B.

document.getElementById("myBtn").addEventListener("click", function() {
 console.log("Clicked!");

});

C. Both A and B

D. Neither A nor B

Answer: C

Explanation: You can use either the `onclick` property or `addEventListener` method. However, `addEventListener` is more flexible.

6. **Which mouse event fires when the mouse pointer enters the boundaries of an element?** A. `mouseout`

B. `mouseenter`

C. `mouseleave`

D. `mouseover`

Answer: D

Explanation: `mouseover` is fired when the mouse pointer enters an element or a child of that element (for direct enters without children, `mouseenter` is used).

7. **Which method stops an event from continuing to bubble up the DOM?**

A. `event.stopPropagation()`

B. `event.stopBubble()`

C. `event.preventDefault()`

D. `event.cancel()`

Answer: A

Explanation: `stopPropagation()` stops the event from further propagation up or down.

8. **What does `e.preventDefault()` do in an event handler?**

A. Cancels the entire script

B. Prevents the default action associated with the event

C. Stops the event from firing

D. Removes the element from the DOM

Answer: B

Explanation: `preventDefault()` prevents the browser's default behavior for that event.

9. **When you bind a function to the `click` event, what is the `this` keyword inside the callback referencing in a standard function (non-arrow) context by default?**

A. The `window` object

B. The element that was clicked

C. The callback function itself

D. An empty object

Answer: B

Explanation: In a non-arrow event handler, `this` refers to the element that fired the event.

10. **How do you call an event listener only once?**

A. By removing it immediately after calling it

B. `element.addEventListener("click", callback, { once: true });`

C. `element.addSingleEventListener("click", callback);`

D. You can't call an event listener only once

Answer: B

Explanation: The third parameter can be an options object with `once: true`, making the listener auto-remove after one call.

11. **Which event is triggered when the user finishes entering text in a text field and the field loses focus?**

A. `blur`

B. `focusout`

C. `keyup`

D. `change`

Answer: D

Explanation: For text input, `change` is typically fired when the element loses focus and its value has changed. (Also note `blur` fires on losing focus, but does not check if the value changed.) 12. **Which property in the event object references the element that triggered the event? A. `event.srcElement`**

B. `event.target`

C. `event.currentTarget`

D. `this`

Answer: B

Explanation: `event.target` is typically the element that initiated the event. `event.currentTarget` can differ if the event is bubbling or if there's capturing.

13. **What is the recommended modern way to handle events in JavaScript?** A. Inline event attributes like `onclick="myFunction()"`

B. `element.onclick = function() { ... };`

C. `element.addEventListener("click", function() { ... });`

D. Using the `on("click")` jQuery method

Answer: C

Explanation: The modern standard approach is `addEventListener`.

14. **Which keyboard event is fired when a key is released?**

A. `keydown`

B. `keypress`

C. `keyup`

D. `releaseKey`

Answer: C

Explanation: `keyup` is triggered when the key is released.

15. **When attaching multiple event listeners of the same type on the same element, they will be executed in which order by default?**

A. Last attached, first executed

B. First attached, first executed

C. Random order

D. They cannot coexist

Answer: B

Explanation: By default, event listeners are called in the order they were registered (first come, first served).

16. **Which of the following is a correct way to define an event handler function?** A.

```
function handleClick(event) {
 console.log("Clicked!");
}
```

B.

```
const handleClick = event => {
 console.log("Clicked!");
}
```

C. Both A and B

D. Neither A nor B

Answer: C

Explanation: Both function declarations and arrow functions are valid ways to define an event handler.

17. **If you use `event.stopPropagation()`, which event phase is prevented?**

A. Capturing

B. Bubbling

C. Target

D. Both capturing and bubbling

Answer: B

Explanation: `stopPropagation()` prevents further bubbling up. `stopImmediatePropagation()` also prevents other listeners on the same element.

18. **Which approach is best for preventing default link navigation on a link with ID `myLink`?** A.

```
myLink.onclick = function() {
 return false;
};
```

B.

```
document.getElementById("myLink").addEventListener("cl
ick", function(e) {
 e.preventDefault();
```

});

C.

myLink.addEventListener("navigate", function() {

 return false;

});

D.

myLink.preventDefault();

Answer: B

Explanation: Using `e.preventDefault()` in the event listener is the standard method to block default navigation.

19. **Which event fires when the DOM is fully loaded (but images not necessarily loaded)?** A. `DOMContentLoaded`

B. `load`

C. `readyStateChange`

D. `windowReady`

Answer: A

Explanation: `DOMContentLoaded` fires when the HTML document is completely loaded and parsed, but images may still be loading. `load` fires after everything, including images, are loaded.

20. **How do you pass additional**

parameters to an event listener's callback? A. You cannot pass extra parameters to an event callback.

B. `element.addEventListener("click", callback(params));`

C. Wrap the callback in another function or use an arrow function to pass parameters. D. Use `event.params = { ... }`

Answer: C

Explanation: You can do something like:

```
element.addEventListener("click", function(e) {
 myFunc(e, "extraParam");
});
```

or use an arrow function for a wrapper.

21. **Which event is commonly used to handle form submission?**

A. `submit`

B. `save`

C. `post`

D. `push`

Answer: A

Explanation: The `submit` event triggers when a form is submitted.

22. **What is the default behavior**

if a form's submit event is not prevented? A. The page reloads and sends form data.

B. Nothing happens.

C. A console log is triggered.

D. An alert appears.

Answer: A

Explanation: By default, form submission reloads the page or navigates to the form's `action` URL.

23. **Which statement is true about inline event handlers like `<button onclick="alert('Hello')">Click</button>`?**

A. They are the recommended standard.

B. They are discouraged in modern practice due to less flexibility.

C. They cannot call JavaScript functions.

D. They are mandatory for all events.

Answer: B

Explanation: Inline event handlers are generally discouraged; separate JS with `addEventListener` is preferred.

24. **How can you listen for the event that fires when an element**

gets focus? A.
`element.addEventListener("focus
", callback)`

B. `element.addEventListener("onfocus", callback)`

C. `element.focusListener = callback;`

D. `element.onFocus = callback;`

Answer: A

Explanation: The correct event type is `"focus"` with `addEventListener("focus", ...)`.

25. What happens if multiple handlers are registered for the same event on the same element? A. Only the last one will run.

B. Only the first one will run.

C. They all run in the order they were added.

D. A conflict causes an error.

Answer: C

Explanation: Multiple event handlers run in sequence, in the order they were added.

Basic Form Handling

Introduction

Forms in HTML collect user input, and JavaScript can process or validate that data before (or after) the form is submitted.

Accessing Form Elements

`document.forms`: A collection of forms in the document.

Form properties: Each form has a `.elements` collection containing its input fields. **Selecting specific inputs**: You can use the standard DOM selection methods (`getElementById`, `querySelector`, etc.).

Handling Form Submission

`submit` event: Fires when the form is submitted. Often used to validate or stop submission using `event.preventDefault()`.

Example:

```
const form = document.getElementById("myForm");
form.addEventListener("submit", function(e) {
 e.preventDefault();
 // validate or process form data
});
```

Retrieving Input Values

For **text inputs**: `inputElement.value`

```
const usernameInput =
document.getElementById("username");
console.log(usernameInput.value);
```

For **checkboxes**: `checkbox.checked`

```
const subscribeCheck =
document.getElementById("subscribe");
```

```javascript
if (subscribeCheck.checked) {
  // user wants to subscribe
}
```

For **radio buttons**: Check `.checked` or loop through a radio group to find which is selected. For **select elements**: `selectElement.value` returns the selected option.

Form Validation

Client-side validation ensures the user input meets criteria before submission. Could involve checking if required fields are filled, or if the email has a valid format, etc.

Example Code

```html
<!DOCTYPE html>
<html>
<head>
  <title>Basic Form Handling</title>
</head>
<body>
  <form id="contactForm">
  <label for="name">Name:</label>
  <input id="name" type="text" name="name"
required><br>
  <label for="email">Email:</label>
```

```html
<input id="email" type="email" name="email"
required><br>
<label><input type="checkbox" id="subscribe"
name="subscribe"> Subscribe</label><br>
<button type="submit">Submit</button>
</form>
<script>
const form = document.getElementById("contactForm");
form.addEventListener("submit", function(e) {
e.preventDefault(); // Stop default submission
const nameValue =
document.getElementById("name").value;
const emailValue =
document.getElementById("email").value;
const isSubscribed =
document.getElementById("subscribe").checked;
console.log("Name:", nameValue);
console.log("Email:", emailValue);
console.log("Subscribed:", isSubscribed);
// You can then do additional validation or an AJAX submit.
});
</script>
</body>
```

</html>

25 Multiple-Choice Questions: Basic Form Handling

1. **Which event is typically used to handle form submission in JavaScript?**

A. `change`

B. `submit`

C. `click`

D. `focus`

Answer: B

Explanation: The `submit` event fires when the form is submitted.

2. **How do you normally prevent a form from refreshing the page upon submit?**

A. `event.returnValue = false;`

B. `event.stopPropagation();`

C. `event.preventDefault();`

D. `form.stop();`

Answer: C

Explanation: `preventDefault()` blocks the default form submission behavior.

3. **What property would you access to get the value of a text input?**

A. `input.text`

B. `input.content`

C. `input.value`

D. `input.getValue()`

Answer: C

Explanation: The `.value` property contains the text input's current value.

4. Which statement is true about HTML form elements in JavaScript?

A. They can only be accessed by `document.forms[0]` syntax.

B. They can be selected using DOM methods like `getElementById`.

C. They must be accessed via jQuery.

D. They automatically post data without JavaScript.

Answer: B

Explanation: You can use any DOM selection method (`getElementById`, `querySelector`, etc.) for form elements.

5. How can you check if a checkbox with `id="subscribe"` is checked?

A. `document.getElementById("subscribe").value`

B. `document.getElementById("subscribe").checked`

C. `document.getElementById("subscribe").isSelected`

D. `document.getElementById("subscribe").selected`

Answer: B

Explanation: The boolean `.checked` property indicates whether a checkbox is checked.

6. **Which form event occurs when a control loses focus?**

A. `blur`

B. `submit`

C. `focus`

D. `change`

Answer: A

Explanation: The `blur` event fires when an element loses focus.

7. **What is the best way to ensure a user has entered a valid email address before submitting a form?**

A. Rely on the HTML `type="email"` attribute alone.

B. Use a client-side validation function checking the input format.

C. Let the server handle it only.

D. Disallow any keystrokes except `@` and `.`

Answer: B

Explanation: While `type="email"` can help, additional client-side validation is often used to check or provide immediate feedback.

8. **Which code snippet correctly retrieves the selected option from a `<select id="colors">`?** A.

const select = document.getElementById("colors");

const selectedValue = select.value;

B.

const selectedValue =

document.getElementById("colors").getAttribute

("selected"); C.

const selectedValue =

document.querySelector("#colors").selectedIndex;

D.

const selectedValue =

document.getElementById("colors").currentOption;

Answer: A

Explanation: `select.value` gives the value of the currently selected option.

9. **Which method is used to get all form elements in a document as a collection?**

A. `document.forms.elements`

B. `document.allForms`

C. `document.forms`

D. `document.all.forms`

Answer: C

Explanation: `document.forms` is an HTMLCollection of all `<form>` elements in the document.

10. **How do you typically handle radio buttons in a form to see which one is selected?** A. `document.getElementById("radio").checked`

B. Loop through all radio inputs with the same `name` attribute and check which has `.checked` set to `true`.

C. They all share the same value.

D. You can't handle radio buttons in JavaScript.

Answer: B

Explanation: For radio buttons, you check which one in a group (same `name`) is checked.

11. **Which property indicates if a form input is required (based on the HTML `required` attribute)?** A. `element.required`

B. `element.isRequired`

C. `element.hasRequired`

D. `element.mandatory`

Answer: A

Explanation: An input's `required` attribute can be accessed via `element.required`.

12. **What happens when you call `form.submit()` in JavaScript?**

A. It triggers the `submit` event but can be prevented with `event.preventDefault()`.

B. It manually submits the form without triggering `submit` event.

C. It does nothing if the form is invalid.

D. It always triggers a page reload with no chance to intercept.

Answer: B

Explanation: Calling `form.submit()` bypasses the `submit` event's default handling. (The event is not fired by a direct `.submit()` call in many browsers.)

13. **How do you get the user's input from a `<textarea>` with `id="notes"`?**

A. `document.getElementById("notes").value`

B. `document.getElementById("notes").textContent`

C. `document.getElementById("notes").innerHTML`

D. `document.getElementById("notes").textValue`

Answer: A

Explanation: A `<textarea>` is an input element, so `.value` is used to retrieve its content.

14. **Which is the correct event listener for intercepting form submission?**

A.

form.addEventListener("submit", (e) => {
 e.preventDefault();

});

B.

form.addEventListener("click", (e) => {

  e.preventDefault();

});

C.

form.addEventListener("onSubmit", (e) => {

  e.preventDefault();

});

D. None of the above

Answer: A

Explanation: The `submit` event is correct, and `e.preventDefault()` stops page reload.

15. **If you do not call `event.preventDefault()` in a form's submit handler, what happens by default?**

A. The user sees an alert.

B. The form data is logged to the console.

C. The form is submitted to the `action` URL or same page.

D. The event is canceled automatically.

Answer: C

Explanation: By default, the form is submitted to its `action` or reloaded if no `action` is specified.

16. **Which property would you check on a**

`<select>` element to see its index of the selected option?

A. `element.index`

B. `element.selectedIndex`

C. `element.currentIndex`

D. `element.valueIndex`

Answer: B

Explanation: `selectElement.selectedIndex` gives the index of the selected option. 17. **How would you programmatically set the value of a text input with ID `username` to `"Alice"`? A.** `document.getElementById("username").textContent = "Alice";`

B. `document.getElementById("username").innerHTML = "Alice";`

C. `document.getElementById("username").value = "Alice";`

D. `document.getElementById("username").content = "Alice";`

Answer: C

Explanation: For text-based form inputs, use `.value`.

18. **Which event triggers each time the user modifies the content of a text**

field? A. `input`

B. `keyup`

C. `change`

D. `blur`

Answer: A

Explanation: The `input` event fires whenever the text changes (including every keystroke).

19. **Which approach is best to handle an invalid form submission?**

A. `alert("Invalid!")` and let the form submit anyway.

B. `form.submit()` forcibly.

C. Check validity in JavaScript, show user feedback, and prevent submission if invalid.

D. Remove the required attributes and let the user guess.

Answer: C

Explanation: Good user experience: check in JavaScript, show helpful messages, and prevent the form from submitting if invalid.

20. **In a typical scenario, how do you handle user input from a form in JavaScript?** A. Collect values from inputs, validate them, possibly send them via AJAX or allow normal submission.

B. Immediately store them in local storage.

C. Replace the entire DOM with a new document.

D. Create a new tab.

Answer: A

Explanation: Common practice is to read input values, validate, and handle them (e.g., send to server).

21. **Which property of a checkbox or radio input indicates whether it is selected?** A. `input.value`

B. `input.status`

C. `input.checked`

D. `input.isTrue`

Answer: C

Explanation: `.checked` is a boolean that indicates if the input is selected (true) or not (false). 22. **What is `document.forms[0]` referring to?**

A. The first form element in the document

B. The first field in the first form

C. The form with ID "0"

D. The last form in the document

Answer: A

Explanation: `document.forms` is a zero-based collection of all forms. `[0]` is the first one.

23. **How do you typically gather all values from a form?**

A. Use `document.forms["myForm"].values`

B. Loop through or select each input and read `.value`

C. `Array.from(form.elements)` then map over `.value`

D. B and C are both valid approaches

Answer: D

Explanation: You can either manually select each input or convert `form.elements` into an array and read `.value`.

24. Which is NOT a valid input type for HTML forms?

A. `type="text"`

B. `type="file"`

C. `type="radio"`

D. `type="picture"`

Answer: D

Explanation: `type="picture"` is not a valid HTML input type.

25. Which approach in JavaScript code can be used to check the validity of a form field that uses HTML5 validation?

A. `input.validity`

B. `input.validate()`

C. `input.isValid`

D. `input.valueCheck`

Answer: A

Explanation: `input.validity` is part of the Constraint Validation API, providing validation states and error messages.

Basic Debugging and Console

Using `console.log`

Introduction

The `console.log` method is one of the most commonly used debugging tools in JavaScript. It allows you to print (or "log") output to your web browser's console or the Node.js console.

Why Use `console.log`?

Debugging: Print variable values or messages at different points in code execution. **Testing**: Quickly check code output without building a complicated UI.

Monitoring: Keep track of certain events or data flows in your application.

Basic Usage

console.log("Hello World!");

This line outputs `"Hello World!"` in the console.

Logging Variables and Expressions

let x = 10;

```
console.log("The value of x is:", x);
// Output: The value of x is: 10
console.log("2 + 2 =", 2 + 2);
// Output: 2 + 2 = 4
```

Logging Multiple Values

```
let name = "Alice";
let age = 25;
console.log("User Info:", name, age);
// Output: User Info: Alice 25
```

You can pass multiple arguments to
`console.log`; they will be displayed separated
by spaces. **Common Console Methods**

`console.log()`: General logging.

`console.error()`: Log an error message
(often displayed with a red icon or text).

`console.warn()`: Log a warning
message (often displayed with a yellow
icon).

`console.info()`: Log an informational message.

`console.table()`: Display data in a tabular format (for
arrays or objects).

`console.trace()`: Show the call stack leading to this log.

Example of `console.table()`:

```
const users = [
```

```
{ id: 1, name: "Alice", role: "Admin" },
{ id: 2, name: "Bob", role: "Editor" },
];
console.table(users);
```

Example of `console.error()`:

```
if (someErrorCondition) {
 console.error("An error occurred!");
}
```

Formatting Console Output

1. **String Substitution**: Some environments allow `%s`, `%d`, `%o` placeholders. js

```
console.log("Name: %s, Age: %d", "Alice", 25);
```

2. **CSS Styling** (Chrome/Firefox):

```
console.log("%cThis is a styled message", "color:blue; font-weight:bold;");
```

Using `console.log` in Different Environments

In the Browser: You'll see the output in the developer console (usually opened via F12, Ctrl+Shift+I, or Cmd+Option+I).

In Node.js: The output appears in the terminal.

Example Code

```
<!DOCTYPE html>
```

```html
<html>
<head>
<title>Console.log Demo</title>
</head>
<body>
<h1>Open the Console</h1>
<script>
console.log("Page is loaded");
let userName = "Alice";
let userAge = 25;
console.log("User name:", userName, "| Age:", userAge);
// Using different console methods
console.warn("This is a warning message!");
console.error("This is an error message!");
// Using table
const fruits = ["Apple", "Banana", "Cherry"];
console.table(fruits);
</script>
</body>
</html>
```

In the above HTML example:

Open your browser console (e.g., in Chrome
or Firefox) to see the logged messages.

Notice the difference between

`console.warn` and `console.error` messages.

25 Multiple-Choice Questions: Using `console.log`

1. Which method is commonly used to display general messages in the JavaScript console? A. `console.info()`

B. `console.log()`

C. `console.warn()`

D. `alert()`

Answer: B

Explanation: `console.log()` is used for general logging messages in the console. 2.

Which of the following is a benefit of using `console.log()`?

A. It halts the program execution.

B. It provides output in the JavaScript console for debugging.

C. It automatically formats all logged data as tables.

D. It triggers an error if used incorrectly.

Answer: B

Explanation: `console.log()` is helpful for outputting information in the console for debugging and inspection.

3. Which console method would you typically use to

display an error message in red text (in most browsers)?

A. `console.log()`

B. `console.error()`

C. `console.warn()`

D. `console.info()`

Answer: B

Explanation: `console.error()` outputs an error message, typically highlighted in red.

4. **What does `console.warn()` do differently than `console.log()`?**

A. It stops the script.

B. It prints a warning message, often with a yellow icon.

C. It logs nothing.

D. It is identical to `console.log()`.

Answer: B

Explanation: `console.warn()` visually distinguishes warnings, often with a yellow icon or text in the console.

5. **Which method would best display data in a structured table format in the console?** A. `console.info()`

B. `console.log()`

C. `console.table()`

D. `console.debug()`

Answer: C

Explanation: `console.table()` formats array or object data as a table.

6. **How can you log multiple values in a single `console.log()` call?**

A. By concatenating them into a single string only.

B. By passing multiple arguments, e.g. `console.log(a, b, c)`.

C. It is not possible to log multiple values.

D. You must use a loop to log each value separately.

Answer: B

Explanation: You can pass multiple arguments to `console.log`, and they will all be displayed.

7. **Which of the following is true about `console.error("Something went wrong")`?** A. It halts the code.

B. It writes an error message to the console, usually highlighted in red.

C. It must be followed by `throw new Error()`.

D. It closes the console.

Answer: B

Explanation: `console.error` highlights the message as an error, but it doesn't halt code execution.

8. **Which console method would you use to show an informational message that is distinct from `console.log()` or `console.error()`?**

A. `console.warn()`

B. `console.info()`

C. `console.debug()`

D. `alert()`

Answer: B

Explanation: `console.info()` is meant for informational messages.

9. **What is the recommended approach to see if a code section is reached during debugging?** A. Use `console.log("Reached here")`.

B. Use `throw new Error("Reached here")`.

C. It's impossible to know.

D. Use `window.alert("Reached here")` only.

Answer: A

Explanation: Placing a `console.log("Reached here")` is a simple and popular technique to confirm the code path.

10. **Which string substitution placeholder inserts a string value in many JavaScript console implementations?**

A. `%s`

B. `%d`

C. `%o`

D. `%c`

Answer: A

Explanation: `%s` is often used for string substitution in `console.log` in certain environments.

11. **What happens if you use `%c` in a `console.log()` in supported browsers?** A. It causes a compile-time error.

B. It inserts a color swatch.

C. It applies CSS styles specified after the format string.

D. It is not recognized by any browsers.

Answer: C

Explanation: `%c` allows you to apply inline CSS styles to the console output in Chrome/Firefox.

12. **What will happen if you call `console.log("Hello");` in Node.js?**

A. It will output "Hello" in the browser console.

B. It will output "Hello" in the Node.js terminal/command prompt.

C. It will show an alert popup.

D. It will throw an error.

Answer: B

Explanation: In Node.js, `console.log` messages appear in the terminal.

13. **Which is a valid way to quickly check the content of an array in the console?** A. `console.table(myArray);`

B. `console.error(myArray);`

C. `console.warn(myArray);`

D. `console.debug(myArray);`

Answer: A

Explanation: `console.table()` can neatly display array or object data in table form.

14. **How do you log an object `user` using `console.log`?**

A. `console.log(user);`

B. `user.console.log();`

C. `console.user(user);`

D. `object.log("user");`

Answer: A

Explanation: `console.log(user);` will display the object details in the console.

15. **Which method can show a stack trace leading to the log call?**

A. `console.trace()`

B. `console.logStack()`

C. `console.infoStack()`

D. `console.backtrace()`

Answer: A

Explanation: `console.trace()` prints the call stack in the console.

16. **What is the difference between** `console.log("Value: " + x)` **and** `console.log("Value:", x)`**?** A. The first uses string concatenation; the second displays multiple arguments separated by spaces.

B. They are identical in every browser.

C. Only the second one is valid syntax.

D. Only the first one works in Node.js.

Answer: A

Explanation: `"Value: " + x` is manual string concatenation. `"Value:", x` is multiple arguments. The console displays them in slightly different ways.

17. **Which of these is NOT a standard console method?**

A. `console.profile()`

B. `console.assert()`

C. `console.clear()`

D. `console.alert()`

Answer: D

Explanation: `console.alert()` is not a standard method. `window.alert()` is separate from console methods.

18. **In browsers, if you type `console.log("Test")` in the DevTools console, what is the result?** A. You get "Test" printed in the console.

B. Nothing happens because `console.log` is disabled in DevTools.

C. You get a popup.

D. It logs "Function" because it's the console.

Answer: A

Explanation: You see the string "Test" printed in the console.

19. **What is a primary reason to use `console.log` statements in code rather than `alert` statements for debugging?**

A. `alert` is never supported in modern browsers.

B. `alert` halts code execution and interrupts user interaction.

C. `console.log` is more complicated to use.

D. `alert` automatically prints the stack trace.

Answer: B

Explanation: `alert` blocks execution until dismissed, which can be disruptive; `console.log` is less intrusive.

20. **What happens if you try to log a variable that does not exist?**

A. The console shows "undefined variable."

B. The console logs `null`.

C. A ReferenceError is thrown.

D. Nothing happens.

Answer: C

Explanation: Accessing an undeclared variable in JavaScript throws a ReferenceError.

21. **Which code snippet logs "2 + 3 = 5" without manually concatenating strings?** A. `console.log("2 + 3 = %s", 2+3);`

B. `console.log("%c2 + 3 = " + (2+3));`

C. `console.info("2 + 3 = "); 2+3;`

D. `console.error("2 + 3 = " + 2+3);`

Answer: A

Explanation: Using `"%s"` with `2+3` will insert the result of `2+3` into the string.

22. **What will `console.warn("Warning", [1, 2, 3])` do?**

A. Throw an error.

B. Log a yellow warning with "Warning" and the array `[1, 2, 3]`.

C. Display an array in a table.

D. Show "Warning: 123".

Answer: B

Explanation: `console.warn` will show a warning icon, the message "Warning", and the array.

23. **Why might you prefer `console.log` over `alert` for debugging large loops?** A. `alert` is faster than `console.log`.

B. `alert` can't display numbers.

C. `alert` could pop up multiple times, blocking the browser.

D. There's no difference; both are the same for large loops.

Answer: C

Explanation: Repeated alerts block the browser and can be annoying, whereas `console.log` is non-blocking.

24. **Which of these statements about `console.log` in Node.js is true?**

A. It displays output in the browser.

B. It displays output in the terminal or command prompt.

C. It automatically writes to a file.

D. It requires a special library to use.

Answer: B

Explanation: In Node.js, `console.log` outputs to the terminal/command prompt. 25. **Which method would you use to clear all messages from the browser console manually?** A. `console.clear();`

B. `console.deleteAll();`

C. `console.reset();`

D. `console.log("clear")`

Answer: A

Explanation: `console.clear()` clears the console output (where supported).

Understanding Errors and Debugging in Browser Developer Tools

Introduction

No matter how experienced you are, **errors** and **bugs** are a natural part of coding. JavaScript developers rely heavily on **browser developer tools** to identify and fix problems.

Types of Errors

1. **Syntax Errors**: Occur when JavaScript code is incorrectly formed (e.g., missing a bracket). js

// Missing parentheses, bracket, or other syntax elements can cause syntax errors

console.log("Hello"

2. **Reference Errors**: Occur when code references a variable or function that doesn't exist in the current scope.

console.log(x); // x is not defined => ReferenceError

3. **Type Errors**: Happen when a value is not of the expected type.

```
let num = 5;
num.toUpperCase(); // TypeError: num.toUpperCase is not
a function
```

4. **Range Errors**: Occur when a value is not within the allowed range (e.g., invalid array length).

5. **Custom Errors**: You can create and throw your own errors.

Locating Errors

Console: The console in the browser's developer tools often logs uncaught exceptions and errors with stack traces pointing to the le and line number.

Debugger: You can open the Sources (Chrome) or Debugger (Firefox) panel to set breakpoints, step through code, and inspect variables.

Using Breakpoints

Line Breakpoints: Pause execution at a specic line of code.

Conditional Breakpoints: Pause execution only if a certain condition is met.

Watch Expressions: Observe variable changes in real time.

Checking Network Requests

In Network tab, you can see if your requests return errors (e.g., `404`, `500`), which might aect your JavaScript logic.

Handling Errors

Try...Catch

```
try {
 // code that may throw an error
} catch (err) {
 console.error("Caught an error:", err);
}
```

Throwing Errors

```
throw new Error("Something went wrong!");
```

Using `console.log()` and `console.error()` to debug.

Example Debugging Steps

1. Open DevTools (F12 or right-click -> "Inspect").

2. Check the Console for error messages and line numbers.

3. Go to Sources/Debugger panel, locate the JS le.

4. Set a Breakpoint near suspicious code.

5. Run/Refresh the page, execution stops at the breakpoint.

6. Inspect Variables in the scope.

7. Step Over / Step Into to move through the code.

8. Watch or log the variable values.

Example Code with an Error

```
<!DOCTYPE html>
<html>
<head>
 <title>Debugging Example</title>
</head>
<body>
 <script>
function greetUser(name) {
console.log("Hello, " + name.toUpperCase());
}
// This will cause a TypeError if name is null or not
a string
let userName = null;
greetUser(userName);
// Check console for the error: "TypeError: Cannot
read properties of null (reading 'toU
pperCase')"
 </script>
</body>
</html>
```

Open the console to see the error.

You can set a breakpoint on the `greetUser` line to see what `userName` is.

25 Multiple-Choice Questions: Understanding

Errors and

Debugging in Browser Developer Tools

1. Which type of JavaScript error occurs when referencing a variable that doesn't exist in the current scope?

A. Syntax Error

B. Reference Error

C. Type Error

D. Range Error

Answer: B

Explanation: A Reference Error appears when a non-existent variable/function is referenced.

2. Which DevTools panel is used to set breakpoints and step through your code?

A. Console

B. Sources (Chrome) / Debugger (Firefox)

C. Network

D. Performance

Answer: B

Explanation: The "Sources" (Chrome) or "Debugger" (Firefox) panel is used for setting breakpoints and stepping through code.

3. When a JavaScript le has a syntax error, where

will you typically see the initial error message?

A. In the HTML itself

B. On the desktop

C. In the browser's console

D. It doesn't appear anywhere

Answer: C

Explanation: A syntax error is usually reported in the console, indicating the le name and line number.

4. What is a breakpoint in the context of debugging?

A. A syntax to end your code execution prematurely

B. A point in the code where execution will pause, allowing inspection of variables

C. A special kind of error

D. A variable that automatically logs data

Answer: B

Explanation: Breakpoints pause code execution at a specic line so you can inspect variables and step through the code.

5. Which statement correctly handles a possible error with try/catch?

A.

```
if (error) {
try {
// code
}
}
```

B.

```
try {
// code that might fail
} catch (err) {
console.error(err);
}
```

C.

```
catch {
// code
}
```

D.

```
throw new Error(); try {}
```

Answer: B

Explanation: A `try { ... } catch(err) { ... }` block is the correct syntax for catching runtime errors in JavaScript.

6. If you see "TypeError: x is not a function" in the console, it indicates...

A. `x` is not dened at all

B. `x` is a string when it should be a number

C. You are attempting to call `x()` but `x` is not a function type

D. You used the wrong variable name

Answer: C

Explanation: A TypeError about "not a function" means you tried to call a property that isn't callable.

7. What is the best initial step if you see an error in your console logs?

A. Disable console logs and run code again

B. Ignore it if it doesn't crash

C. Read the message and check the le/line number indicated

D. Immediately reinstall Node.js

Answer: C

Explanation: Read the console message carefully, it often provides le name and line number for the error.

8. Which type of error is thrown if you try to set an array length to a negative number?

A. Reference Error

B. Syntax Error

C. Type Error

D. Range Error

Answer: D

Explanation: Trying to set an invalid length on an array leads to a Range Error.

9. In browser DevTools, what does the 'Network' panel help you debug?

A. The code's syntax errors

B. HTTP requests and responses

C. Code coverage

D. Local variable values

Answer: B

Explanation: The Network panel shows HTTP requests, statuses, response times, etc.

10. Which statement is true about console error messages?

A. They are invisible to developers.

B. They always crash the browser.

C. They provide helpful clues like line numbers and stack traces.

D. They must be enabled in production.

Answer: C

Explanation: Console error messages typically show

le, line number, and sometimes a stack trace.

11. What is the result of throwing a custom error with `throw new Error("Custom message");`?

A. A console log is added but no eect on code.

B. Code execution halts unless it's caught in a try/catch.

C. It creates a syntax error.

D. It transforms into a `ReferenceError`.

Answer: B

Explanation: Throwing an error halts normal ow unless there's a `try/catch` to handle it.

12. Which method helps track variable changes in real time when the code is paused at a breakpoint?

A. Setting a watch expression in the DevTools debugger

B. Using `alert(variable)` repeatedly

C. Adding more console.log statements

D. None of the above

Answer: A

Explanation: In DevTools, you can use "Watch expressions" to monitor variables during breakpoint pauses.

13. Which is NOT a common JavaScript error type?

A. Syntax Error

B. Type Error

C. Memory Error

D. Reference Error

Answer: C

Explanation: "Memory Error" is not typically classied as a built-in JavaScript error type.

14. You have a line of code that says `user.name.toUpperCase()`. The console error says `Cannot read property 'toUpperCase' of undefined`. Which is likely the cause?

A. `user` is undened or `user.name` is undened.

B. `toUpperCase` is not a function in JavaScript.

C. The code has a syntax error.

D. toUpperCase should be spelled `toUppercase`.

Answer: A

Explanation: The error indicates `user.name` might be `undefined`, so `undefined.toUpperCase()` is invalid.

15. How do you open the Browser Developer

Tools in most browsers?

A. Right-click -> "Save As..."

B. F12 or Ctrl+Shift+I (Cmd+Option+I on Mac)

C. Double-click the tab bar

D. It's not possible

Answer: B

Explanation: F12 or the respective shortcuts open Developer Tools in many browsers.

16. What does the 'pause on exceptions' feature do in the debugger?

A. Pauses the code on every console.log statement

B. Pauses only on network failures

C. Pauses execution whenever an exception is thrown (if desired, even for caught exceptions)

D. Pauses the code on successful requests

Answer: C

Explanation: 'Pause on exceptions' stops the code precisely when an error occurs, helping to debug the cause.

17. In a debugger, what does "Step Into" do?

A. Skips executing the current function entirely

B. Executes the rest of the function instantly

C. Steps into the next function call, letting you debug inside that function

D. Moves to the next breakpoint ignoring function calls

Answer: C

Explanation: "Step Into" allows you to go into the function that is about to be called line by line.

18. Which statement about DevTools is correct?

A. They are only for viewing HTML.

B. They can help with inspecting CSS, debugging JavaScript, and monitoring network requests.

C. They are third-party tools not included with browsers.

D. They only work when you're oine.

Answer: B

Explanation: DevTools provide a suite of features for debugging code, inspecting DOM, network analysis, and more.

19. Which approach can help you debug a function that's returning an unexpected result?

A. Insert `console.log` statements inside the function to observe variable values.

B. Throw a custom error at the end of the function.

C. Hide the function code.

D. Always rename the function.

Answer: A

Explanation: Logging inside the function reveals intermediate values and helps isolate the problem.

20. If your code references `document.getElementById("submitBtn")`, but the element doesn't exist yet in the DOM, you might get:

A. A syntax error

B. A reference error or `null`

C. A type error

D. An innite loop

Answer: B

Explanation: `document.getElementById("submitBtn")` could return `null` if the element doesn't exist. Accessing a property on `null` might cause a TypeError.

21. What does the stack trace in an error message show?

A. A complete list of global variables

B. The function call path that led to the error

C. The browser's system information

D. The contents of your memory

Answer: B

Explanation: A stack trace shows the series of function calls (call stack) that led to the error.

22. Which tool can help you see if your code or resources failed to load from the server (e.g., 404 error)?

A. Console panel

B. Network panel

C. Elements panel

D. Sources panel

Answer: B

Explanation: The Network panel shows HTTP request statuses like 200, 404, 500, etc.

23. When debugging, how can you watch a variable's changing value over multiple lines of code without adding multiple console.logs?

A. Use "Watch Expressions" in DevTools.

B. You must add multiple console.logs anyway.

C. Add an alert at each line.

D. Rename the variable after each line.

Answer: A

Explanation: "Watch Expressions" allow you to track a variable's value as you step through code.

24. Which of the following would cause a SyntaxError in JavaScript?

A. Using an object's property that doesn't exist.

B. Misspelling a function name.

C. Missing a curly brace or parenthesis.

D. Logging a variable.

Answer: C

Explanation: SyntaxErrors occur due to invalid code syntax, like missing braces or parentheses.

25. How can you handle a runtime error gracefully so it doesn't crash your entire script?

A. Put the code in a comment.

B. Use a `try { ... } catch(e) { ... }` block to catch the error.

C. Never use functions.

D. It's impossible to handle runtime errors.

Answer: B

Explanation: A `try/catch` block can handle errors without stopping the entire script execution.

JavaScript Basics Coding Exercises

1. Variables and Constants

Exercise 1: Declare and Initialize Variables

Task: Declare a variable age and initialize it with your age. Then, log it to the console.

```
let age = 25;
console.log(age); // Output: 25
```

Exercise 2: Change Variable Value

Task: Declare a variable score, set it to 50, then update it to 75 and log both values.

```
let score = 50;
console.log(score); // Output: 50
score = 75;
console.log(score); // Output: 75
```

Exercise 3: Use Constants

Task: Declare a constant PI with the value 3.14 and attempt to change its value. Observe what happens.

```
const PI = 3.14;
console.log(PI); // Output: 3.14
// PI = 3.14159; // Error: Assignment to constant variable.
```

Exercise 4: Variable Naming

Task: Declare variables with different valid naming conventions (camelCase, snake_case, etc.) and log them.

```
let firstName = "John";
let last_name = "Doe";
let Age2024 = 30;
console.log(firstName, last_name, Age2024); // Output: John Doe 30
```

Exercise 5: Variable Types

Task: Declare variables of different types (string, number, boolean) and log their types using typeof.

```
let name = "Alice";
let height = 170;
let isStudent = true;
console.log(typeof name);     // Output: string
console.log(typeof height);   // Output: number
console.log(typeof isStudent); // Output: boolean
```

2. Data Types (Strings, Numbers, Booleans, etc.)

Exercise 1: String Concatenation

Task: Combine two strings firstName and lastName into a full name.

```
let firstName = "Jane";
```

```
let lastName = "Smith";

let fullName = firstName + " " + lastName;

console.log(fullName); // Output: Jane Smith
```

Exercise 2: Number Operations

Task: Perform addition, subtraction, multiplication, and division on two numbers and log the results.

```
let a = 10;

let b = 5;

console.log(a + b); // 15

console.log(a - b); // 5

console.log(a * b); // 50

console.log(a / b); // 2
```

Exercise 3: Boolean Logic

Task: Create two boolean variables and use logical operators (&&, ||, !) to combine them.

```
let isSunny = true;

let isWeekend = false;

console.log(isSunny && isWeekend); // false

console.log(isSunny || isWeekend); // true

console.log(!isSunny);        // false
```

Exercise 4: Array Data Type

Task: Create an array of fruits and access the second fruit.

```
let fruits = ["Apple", "Banana", "Cherry"];
```

```
console.log(fruits[1]); // Output: Banana
```

Exercise 5: Object Data Type

Task: Create an object person with properties name, age, and isStudent, then log each property.

```
let person = {
  name: "Emily",
  age: 22,
  isStudent: true
};
console.log(person.name);     // Output: Emily
console.log(person.age);      // Output: 22
console.log(person.isStudent); // Output: true
```

3. Basic Operators (Arithmetic, Comparison, Logical)

Exercise 1: Arithmetic Operator Precedence

Task: Calculate the expression 5 + 3 * 2 and explain the result.

```
let result = 5 + 3 * 2;
console.log(result); // Output: 11
// Multiplication has higher precedence, so 3*2 is evaluated
first.
```

Exercise 2: Comparison Operators

Task: Compare two variables using == and === and observe the differences.

```
let x = 10;
let y = "10";
console.log(x == y);  // Output: true (loose equality)
console.log(x === y); // Output: false (strict equality)
```

Exercise 3: Increment and Decrement

Task: Use ++ and -- operators on a variable and log the results.

```
let count = 5;
count++;
console.log(count); // Output: 6
count--;
console.log(count); // Output: 5
```

Exercise 4: Logical Operators in Conditions

Task: Use logical operators to check if a number is between 10 and 20.

```
let num = 15;
if (num > 10 && num < 20) {
  console.log("Number is between 10 and 20"); // This will execute
}
```

Exercise 5: Ternary Operator

Task: Use a ternary operator to assign a message based on a boolean variable.

let isMember = true;

let message = isMember ? "Welcome, member!" : "Please sign up.";

console.log(message); // Output: Welcome, member!

4. Conditional Statements (if, else, switch)

Exercise 1: Basic if Statement

Task: Check if a number is positive and log a message.

let number = 7;

if (number > 0) {

  console.log("The number is positive."); // This will execute

}

Exercise 2: if-else Statement

Task: Determine if a user is old enough to vote (18+) and log appropriate messages.

let age = 16;

if (age >= 18) {

  console.log("You can vote.");

} else {

  console.log("You are too young to vote."); // This will execute

```
}
```

Exercise 3: if-else if-else Statement

Task: Assign a grade based on a score using multiple conditions.

```
let score = 85;
if (score >= 90) {
  console.log("Grade: A");
} else if (score >= 80) {
  console.log("Grade: B"); // This will execute
} else if (score >= 70) {
  console.log("Grade: C");
} else {
  console.log("Grade: F");
}
```

Exercise 4: Switch Statement

Task: Use a switch statement to log the day of the week based on a number (1-7).

```
let day = 3;
switch (day) {
  case 1:
    console.log("Monday");
    break;
  case 2:
```

```javascript
    console.log("Tuesday");
    break;
  case 3:
    console.log("Wednesday"); // This will execute
    break;
  case 4:
    console.log("Thursday");
    break;
  case 5:
    console.log("Friday");
    break;
  case 6:
    console.log("Saturday");
    break;
  case 7:
    console.log("Sunday");
    break;
  default:
    console.log("Invalid day");
}
```

Exercise 5: Nested Conditionals

Task: Check if a number is even and greater than 10.

```javascript
let num = 12;
if (num > 10) {
```

```javascript
if (num % 2 === 0) {
  console.log("Number is even and greater than 10."); // This will execute
  }
}
```

5. Loops (for, while, do...while)

Exercise 1: For Loop - Counting

Task: Use a for loop to count from 1 to 5 and log each number.

```javascript
for (let i = 1; i <= 5; i++) {
  console.log(i);
}
// Output: 1, 2, 3, 4, 5
```

Exercise 2: While Loop - Countdown

Task: Use a while loop to count down from 5 to 1.

```javascript
let count = 5;
while (count > 0) {
  console.log(count);
  count--;
}
// Output: 5, 4, 3, 2, 1
```

Exercise 3: Do...While Loop - At Least Once

Task: Use a do...while loop to execute a block at least once, even if the condition is false.

```
let x = 0;
do {
  console.log("This will print once.");
} while (x > 0);
// Output: This will print once.
```

Exercise 4: Loop Through an Array

Task: Use a for loop to iterate through an array of colors and log each color.

```
let colors = ["Red", "Green", "Blue"];
for (let i = 0; i < colors.length; i++) {
  console.log(colors[i]);
}
// Output: Red, Green, Blue
```

Exercise 5: Break and Continue

Task: Use break to exit a loop when a condition is met and continue to skip an iteration.

```
for (let i = 1; i <= 5; i++) {
  if (i === 3) {
    continue; // Skip when i is 3
  }
  if (i === 5) {
```

```
    break; // Exit loop when i is 5
  }
  console.log(i);
}
// Output: 1, 2, 4
```

6. Basic Functions (Function Declaration and Invocation)

Exercise 1: Function Declaration and Call

Task: Declare a function greet that logs "Hello, World!" and call it.

```
function greet() {
  console.log("Hello, World!");
}
greet(); // Output: Hello, World!
```

Exercise 2: Function with Parameters

Task: Create a function add that takes two numbers and returns their sum.

```
function add(a, b) {
  return a + b;
}
let sum = add(5, 3);
console.log(sum); // Output: 8
```

Exercise 3: Function with Return Value

Task: Write a function isEven that returns true if a number is even, else false.

```
function isEven(number) {
  return number % 2 === 0;
}
console.log(isEven(4)); // Output: true
console.log(isEven(7)); // Output: false
```

Exercise 4: Anonymous Function and Arrow Function

Task: Assign an anonymous function and an arrow function to variables and invoke them.

```
// Anonymous function
let sayHi = function() {
  console.log("Hi!");
};
sayHi(); // Output: Hi!
// Arrow function
let sayBye = () => {
  console.log("Bye!");
};
sayBye(); // Output: Bye!
```

Exercise 5: Function Scope

Task: Demonstrate variable scope by declaring a variable inside and outside a function.

```
let globalVar = "I am global";
function scopeTest() {
  let localVar = "I am local";
  console.log(globalVar); // Output: I am global
  console.log(localVar);  // Output: I am local
}
scopeTest();
console.log(globalVar); // Output: I am global
// console.log(localVar); // Error: localVar is not defined
```

JavaScript DOM Exercises

1. Selecting Elements (getElementById, querySelector, etc.)

Exercise 1: Select Element by ID

Task: Use getElementById to select a paragraph with the ID myParagraph and log its text content.

HTML:

```
<p id="myParagraph">This is a paragraph.</p>
```

JavaScript:

```javascript
let paragraph = document.getElementById("myParagraph");
console.log(paragraph.textContent); // Output: This is a
paragraph.
```

Exercise 2: Select Elements by Class Name

Task: Use getElementsByClassName to select all elements with the class item and log the number of elements selected.

HTML:
```html
<ul>
  <li class="item">Item 1</li>
  <li class="item">Item 2</li>
  <li class="item">Item 3</li>
</ul>
```

JavaScript:
```javascript
let items = document.getElementsByClassName("item");
console.log(items.length); // Output: 3
```

Exercise 3: Select Elements Using querySelector

Task: Use querySelector to select the first <h1> element and change its color to blue.

HTML:
```html
<h1>Welcome!</h1>
<h1>Enjoy your stay.</h1>
```

JavaScript:
```javascript
let header = document.querySelector("h1");
header.style.color = "blue";
```

Exercise 4: Select Elements Using querySelectorAll

Task: Use querySelectorAll to select all buttons with the class btn and log their inner text.

HTML:

```html
<button class="btn">Save</button>
<button class="btn">Cancel</button>
<button class="btn">Delete</button>
```

JavaScript:

```javascript
let buttons = document.querySelectorAll(".btn");
buttons.forEach((button) => {
  console.log(button.innerText);
});
// Output:
// Save
// Cancel
// Delete
```

Exercise 5: Select Nested Elements

Task: Use querySelector to select the <span> inside a <div> with the ID container and update its text.

HTML:

```html
<div id="container">
  <span>Old Text</span>
```

```
</div>
```

JavaScript:

```
let span = document.querySelector("#container span");
span.textContent = "New Text";
console.log(span.textContent); // Output: New Text
```

2. Changing Element Content and Attributes

Exercise 1: Change Text Content

Task: Select a <div> with the ID message and change its text to "Hello, World!".

HTML:

```
<div id="message">Original Message</div>
```

JavaScript:

```
let messageDiv = document.getElementById("message");
messageDiv.textContent = "Hello, World!";
```

Exercise 2: Update Inner HTML

Task: Select a <div> with the class container and insert a new <p> element inside it using innerHTML.

HTML:

```
<div class="container">
  <p>Existing paragraph.</p>
</div>
```

JavaScript:

```
let container = document.querySelector(".container");
container.innerHTML += "<p>New paragraph added.</p>";
```

Exercise 3: Change Element Style

Task: Select a button with the ID myButton and change its background color to green and text color to white.

HTML:

```
<button id="myButton">Click Me!</button>
```

JavaScript:

```
let button = document.getElementById("myButton");
button.style.backgroundColor = "green";
button.style.color = "white";
```

Exercise 4: Modify Attributes

Task: Select an image with the ID myImage and change its src and alt attributes.

HTML:

```
<img id="myImage" src="old-image.jpg" alt="Old Image">
```

JavaScript:

```
let img = document.getElementById("myImage");
img.setAttribute("src", "new-image.jpg");
img.setAttribute("alt", "New Image");
```

Exercise 5: Toggle CSS Classes

Task: Select a <div> with the class box and toggle the class active when a button is clicked.

```
```

HTML:

```html
<div class="box">I am a box.</div>
<button id="toggleButton">Toggle Active</button>
```

JavaScript:

```javascript
let box = document.querySelector(".box");
let toggleButton =
document.getElementById("toggleButton");
toggleButton.addEventListener("click", () => {
  box.classList.toggle("active");
});
```

CSS (for visualization):

```css
.active {
  background-color: yellow;
}
```

3. Event Listeners and Event Handling

Exercise 1: Click Event Listener

Task: Add a click event listener to a button that alerts "Button Clicked!".

HTML:

```html
<button id="alertButton">Click Me</button>
```

JavaScript:

```javascript
let alertButton = document.getElementById("alertButton");
alertButton.addEventListener("click", () => {
  alert("Button Clicked!");
```

```
});
```

Exercise 2: Mouseover and Mouseout Events

Task: Change the background color of a <div> when the mouse hovers over it and revert when the mouse leaves.

HTML:

```html
<div id="hoverDiv" style="width:200px; height:100px;
background-color:lightblue;">
  Hover over me!
</div>
```

JavaScript:

```javascript
let hoverDiv = document.getElementById("hoverDiv");
hoverDiv.addEventListener("mouseover", () => {
  hoverDiv.style.backgroundColor = "lightgreen";
});
hoverDiv.addEventListener("mouseout", () => {
  hoverDiv.style.backgroundColor = "lightblue";
});
```

Exercise 3: Input Event Listener

Task: Add an event listener to an input field that logs its current value whenever the user types.

HTML:

```html
<input type="text" id="textInput" placeholder="Type
something...">
```

JavaScript:

```
let textInput = document.getElementById("textInput");
textInput.addEventListener("input", (event) => {
  console.log(event.target.value);
});
```

Exercise 4: Form Submission Handling

Task: Prevent the default form submission and log the input value instead.

HTML:

```
<form id="myForm">
  <input type="text" id="nameInput" placeholder="Enter your name">
  <button type="submit">Submit</button>
</form>
```

JavaScript:

```
let form = document.getElementById("myForm");
let nameInput = document.getElementById("nameInput");
form.addEventListener("submit", (event) => {
  event.preventDefault();
  console.log("Name:", nameInput.value);
});
```

Exercise 5: Keypress Event Listener

Task: Detect when the "Enter" key is pressed in an input field and log a message.

HTML:

```html
<input type="text" id="enterInput" placeholder="Press
Enter...">
```

JavaScript:

```javascript
let enterInput = document.getElementById("enterInput");
enterInput.addEventListener("keypress", (event) => {
  if (event.key === "Enter") {
    console.log("Enter key was pressed!");
  }
});
```

4. Basic Form Handling

Exercise 1: Retrieve Form Data

Task: Create a form with inputs for name and email. On submission, retrieve and log the entered values.

HTML:

```html
<form id="userForm">
  <label for="name">Name:</label>
  <input type="text" id="name" required><br><br>
  <label for="email">Email:</label>
  <input type="email" id="email" required><br><br>
  <button type="submit">Submit</button>
</form>
```

JavaScript:

```
let userForm = document.getElementById("userForm");
let nameInput = document.getElementById("name");
let emailInput = document.getElementById("email");
userForm.addEventListener("submit", (event) => {
  event.preventDefault();
  let name = nameInput.value;
  let email = emailInput.value;
  console.log("Name:", name);
  console.log("Email:", email);
});
```

Exercise 2: Validate Form Fields

Task: Ensure that the password and confirm password fields match before allowing form submission.

HTML:

```
<form id="passwordForm">
  <label for="password">Password:</label>
  <input type="password" id="password" required><br><br>
  <label for="confirmPassword">Confirm Password:</label>
  <input type="password" id="confirmPassword"
required><br><br>
  <button type="submit">Register</button>
</form>
<p id="error" style="color:red;"></p>
```

JavaScript:

```
let passwordForm =
document.getElementById("passwordForm");
let password = document.getElementById("password");
let confirmPassword =
document.getElementById("confirmPassword");
let error = document.getElementById("error");
passwordForm.addEventListener("submit", (event) => {
  event.preventDefault();
  if (password.value !== confirmPassword.value) {
    error.textContent = "Passwords do not match!";
  } else {
    error.textContent = "";
    console.log("Registration successful!");
    // Proceed with form submission or further processing
  }
});
```

Exercise 3: Dynamically Add Form Fields

Task: Add a button that, when clicked, adds a new input field to the form.

HTML:

```
<form id="dynamicForm">
  <label for="item1">Item 1:</label>
  <input type="text" id="item1" name="item1"><br><br>
```

```html
<button type="button" id="addItem">Add Another
Item</button><br><br>
  <button type="submit">Submit</button>
</form>
```

JavaScript:

```javascript
let addItemButton = document.getElementById("addItem");
let dynamicForm =
document.getElementById("dynamicForm");
let itemCount = 1;
addItemButton.addEventListener("click", () => {
  itemCount++;
  let label = document.createElement("label");
  label.setAttribute("for", `item${itemCount}`);
  label.textContent = `Item ${itemCount}:`;
  let input = document.createElement("input");
  input.type = "text";
  input.id = `item${itemCount}`;
  input.name = `item${itemCount}`;
  dynamicForm.insertBefore(label, addItemButton);
  dynamicForm.insertBefore(input, addItemButton);
  dynamicForm.insertBefore(document.createElement("br"),
addItemButton);
  dynamicForm.insertBefore(document.createElement("br"),
addItemButton);
```

});

Exercise 4: Display Form Data in the DOM

Task: After form submission, display the entered data below the form instead of logging it to the console.

HTML:

```
<form id="displayForm">
 <label for="username">Username:</label>
 <input type="text" id="username" required><br><br>
 <label for="useremail">Email:</label>
 <input type="email" id="useremail" required><br><br>
 <button type="submit">Submit</button>
</form>
<div id="displayData"></div>
```

JavaScript:

```
let displayForm = document.getElementById("displayForm");
let username = document.getElementById("username");
let useremail = document.getElementById("useremail");
let displayData = document.getElementById("displayData");
displayForm.addEventListener("submit", (event) => {
 event.preventDefault();
 displayData.innerHTML = `
  <h3>Submitted Data:</h3>
  <p><strong>Username:</strong> ${username.value}</p>
```

```
<p><strong>Email:</strong> ${useremail.value}</p>
`;
});
```

Exercise 5: Reset Form Fields

Task: Add a "Reset" button to the form that clears all input fields when clicked.

HTML:

```
<form id="resetForm">
  <label for="firstname">First Name:</label>
  <input type="text" id="firstname"><br><br>
  <label for="lastname">Last Name:</label>
  <input type="text" id="lastname"><br><br>
  <button type="submit">Submit</button>
  <button type="button" id="resetButton">Reset</button>
</form>
```

JavaScript:

```
let resetButton = document.getElementById("resetButton");
let resetForm = document.getElementById("resetForm");
resetButton.addEventListener("click", () => {
  resetForm.reset();
});
```

Summary

These exercises cover essential aspects of interacting with the Document Object Model (DOM) and handling forms using

JavaScript. By completing them, you'll gain practical experience in:

- **Selecting Elements:** Using various methods like getElementById, getElementsByClassName, querySelector, and querySelectorAll to access HTML elements.

- **Changing Element Content and Attributes:** Modifying text, HTML content, styles, and attributes of elements dynamically.

- **Event Listeners and Event Handling:** Responding to user interactions such as clicks, mouse movements, and keyboard events.

- **Basic Form Handling:** Managing form submissions, validating input, dynamically adding form fields, and displaying form data.

Feel free to experiment with these examples and modify them to suit your learning needs. Practicing these exercises will enhance your understanding of how JavaScript interacts with HTML to create dynamic and interactive web pages.

Conclusion

Congratulations on reaching the conclusion of **JavaScript Code Foundations for Beginners**! By completing this book, you have taken a significant step toward mastering the fundamentals of programming with JavaScript. More importantly, you have gained the confidence and skills to tackle real-world coding challenges and build your own projects.

Reflecting on Your Journey

Throughout this book, you've explored key concepts and applied them through hands-on exercises. From understanding variables and data types to mastering loops, functions, and DOM manipulation, each chapter was designed to build your knowledge incrementally. By working through these exercises, you've achieved several important milestones:

1. **Developed Problem-Solving Skills:** You've learned to think like a programmer, breaking problems into manageable pieces and devising logical solutions.

2. **Built a Solid Foundation:** The concepts covered in this book form the building blocks of modern programming. Whether you're pursuing web development, backend programming, or app development, these skills will serve you well.

3. **Applied Knowledge:** Beyond theory, you've practiced coding in ways that mimic real-world scenarios, giving you practical experience that's immediately applicable.

4. **Gained Confidence:** Each challenge you overcame has prepared you to tackle more complex problems and continue your learning journey.

The Next Steps in Your Coding Adventure

Learning to code is a lifelong process, and this book marks the beginning of that journey. Here are some ways to continue growing as a developer:

1. **Build Projects:** Use the skills you've learned to create your own applications. Start small—a simple calculator, a to-do list app, or a portfolio website—and gradually take on bigger projects.

2. **Explore Advanced Topics:** Dive deeper into JavaScript and explore areas like asynchronous programming, APIs, frameworks (such as React or Vue), and backend development with Node.js.

3. **Practice Regularly:** Coding is a skill that improves with repetition. Solve coding challenges on platforms like CodeWars, HackerRank, or LeetCode to sharpen your abilities.

4. **Contribute to Open Source:** Join the developer community by contributing to open-source projects.

It's a great way to learn, collaborate, and showcase your skills.

5. **Learn Additional Languages:** Expand your skill set by learning other programming languages, such as Python, Java, or C#. Understanding multiple languages makes you a versatile developer.

Final Thoughts

As you close this book, remember that coding is more than a technical skill—it's a way of thinking and creating. The journey you've started is one filled with opportunities to innovate, solve problems, and bring your ideas to life. The foundation you've built here will support you as you explore more advanced topics and embark on your next projects. Keep challenging yourself, stay curious, and never stop learning. The world of programming is vast, and there's always something new to discover.

Thank you for choosing **JavaScript Code Foundations for Beginners** as your guide. It has been a privilege to accompany you on this journey, and we wish you all the success in your future coding endeavors.

Code Foundations Cheat Sheet

1. Variables and Constants

Variables:

let age = 25; // Reassignable

var name = "John"; // Older syntax, avoid in modern JS

Constants:

const PI = 3.14; // Cannot be reassigned

2. Data Types

- **Primitive Data Types:**
    - String: "Hello"
    - Number: 42
    - Boolean: true or false
    - Null: null
    - Undefined: undefined
    - Symbol: Symbol('unique')

Type Checking:

typeof "Hello"; // "string"

typeof 42; // "number"

3. Basic Operators

Arithmetic: +, -, *, /, %

let sum = 5 + 3; // 8

Comparison: ==, ===, !=, !==, >, <, >=, <=

5 === "5"; // false

Logical: &&, ||, !

true && false; // false

4. Conditional Statements

If-Else:

```
if (age > 18) {
  console.log("Adult");
} else {
  console.log("Minor");
}
```

Switch:

```
switch (day) {
  case 1: console.log("Monday"); break;
  default: console.log("Invalid day");
}
```

5. Loops

For Loop:

```
for (let i = 0; i < 5; i++) {
  console.log(i);
}
```

While Loop:

```
let count = 0;
while (count < 5) {
  console.log(count);
  count++;
}
```

Do-While Loop:

```
do {
  console.log("Run once");
} while (false);
```

6. Functions

Declaration:

```
function greet(name) {
  return `Hello, ${name}`;
}
```

Arrow Function:

```
const greet = (name) => `Hello, ${name}`;
```

7. Selecting Elements

By ID:

```
let element = document.getElementById("myId");
```

By Class/Tag:

```
let elements =
document.getElementsByClassName("myClass");
```

Using Query Selectors:

```
let element = document.querySelector(".myClass");
let elements = document.querySelectorAll(".myClass");
```

8. Changing Element Content and Attributes

Change Content:

```
element.textContent = "New Text";
```

element.innerHTML = "Bold Text";

Modify Attributes:

element.setAttribute("src", "image.jpg");

element.classList.add("active");

9. Event Listeners

Adding Events:

```
button.addEventListener("click", () => {
  console.log("Button clicked");
});
```

- **Mouse Events:**
    - mouseover, mouseout
- **Keyboard Events:**
    - keypress, keyup, keydown

10. Basic Form Handling

Prevent Form Submission:

```
form.addEventListener("submit", (event) => {
  event.preventDefault();
});
```

Access Input Values:

let value = inputField.value;

Validate Input:

```
if (!email.includes("@")) {
  console.log("Invalid email");
}
```

Common Pitfalls

1. **Global Variables:** Avoid using var to prevent scope issues.

2. **Loose Equality (==):** Prefer strict equality (===) to avoid unexpected type coercion.

3. **Forgetting Event Binding:** Always attach events dynamically for flexibility.

Quick Tips

- Use console.log liberally to debug.
- Modularize code into reusable functions.
- Keep your code DRY (Don't Repeat Yourself).
- Test often and iterate!